The Death of Doctor Gilmore's Wife

Gary Ludwig

Basket Road Press, Incorporated
Harrisburg, PA USA

First Edition

This book is distributed internationally
and is available on the Internet and wherever books are sold.

For information or to order additional books contact:
info@basketroadpress.com

WWW.BASKETROADPRESS.COM

To Beth:
You're always on my mind.

To Christine, Daniel, Elijah, and Sadie

In memory of Marcia and John,
Mom and Dad

About the Author

Gary Ludwig began his career in radio, working as a producer, copywriter, news and sports writer, marketing manager, morning radio host, and country music disc jockey.

He began working in advertising, and before that was a columnist for the nationally circulated weekly auto-racing tabloid *Illustrated Speedway News* and at the same time anchored *Speedsport Commentary Radio Network* news segments heard on numerous radio stations reaching listeners in parts of Pennsylvania, Maryland, and New York.

Later he founded a regional magazine in central Pennsylvania, writing commentary and feature articles while serving as publisher.

He wrote a series of magazine articles about *The Blue Eyed Six*, a nineteenth-century Pennsylvania murder, later published in booklet form, and is interviewed in the Kreider Brothers–produced documentary film about the crime.

Ludwig's gritty crime-and-romance novel *Mexico Road* was published in 2006, followed by fantasy novel *The Angels and Demons of Hamlin* in 2008. He is the author of the biography of Indianapolis 500 auto-racing legend *Tommy Hinnershitz,* published in 2009.

He continues to reside in Pennsylvania and works as a writer of fiction and nonfiction.

Additional books
by Gary Ludwig

Mexico Road: A crime & romance novel
The Angels & Demons of Hamlin: A fantasy novel
The Blue Eyed Six: A historical narrative
Tommy Hinnershitz, The Life & Times of an Auto Racing Legend:
A sports biography

Table of Contents

Preface...13

Introduction 21

Chapter 1 – Death at the Gilmore House 31

Chapter 2 – The Interrogation................................39

Chapter 3 – The Aftermath....................................75

Chapter 4 – The Murder Charge 83

Chapter 5 – The Defender.....................................89

Chapter 6 – The Hearing.......................................97

Chapter 7 – The Emergency Room Doctor................131

Chapter 8 – The Importance of Toxicology 143

Chapter 9 – Expert Testimony 155

Chapter 10 – More Witnesses 177

Chapter 11 – The Slow Journey to Justice Begins.......195

Chapter 12 – The Trial 217

Chapter 13 – The Verdict 253

Principal Characters

Emmanuel Dimitriou
Gilmore defense attorney

Thomas Dougherty
Muhlenberg police officer

Doctor William Glosser
Berks County coroner

Charles Haddad
Special prosecutor

Doctor John Keith
Doctor who performed autopsy

Doctor George Kershner
Emergency room doctor

Charles Mackin, Jr.
Chief deputy attorney general

Barrie Pease
Pennsylvania state trooper

Doctor Fredrick Rieders
Head of testing laboratory

Forrest Schaeffer
Presiding county judge

Harley Smith
Muhlenberg police chief

Stuart Suss
Assistant district attorney

Preface

Court testimony appears as spoken.

When the tragedy occurred, family, friends, patients, and contemporaries—all those who were considered advocates for Doctor Irvin Gilmore—stepped forward to support him. He was a man who had always shown good character, and more importantly was a doctor who possessed a profound dedication to his patients. He still made house calls years after that passed away as a common practice—that was one of the reasons he had become a celebrity. Now there was another reason: police said he murdered his wife.

There were disparagers as well who convinced themselves that he intentionally killed her. Typically, most passed judgment either way based on the limited time and space the press could spend to report the story.

Many others, mostly people who didn't know him, were simply following the guilty or not-guilty story to watch justice meted out. The cynical and apathetic watched to see if a miscarriage of justice unfolded. It wasn't easy to support him once the police investigators declared him to be the cold-blooded killer of his beautiful 36-year-old wife Patricia, 22 years his junior.

Anyone who attempts to search at long last for finality and to reach personal conclusions about the tragic death of Patricia Gilmore must first tackle the tedious task of reading the case's exacting details. This book can be the tool to disentangle the police investigation, the roles medical personnel played, the maneuvers of the prosecutors and defense counsel, the conduct of the defendant and every other participator, and of course the boundless judicial process that began the minute Patty died.

One irrefutable fact exists: Patty Gilmore died tragically in the prime of her life, denied perhaps fifty years of prolonged existence. She missed her turn to be happy, content, and productive, and to mature and age with dignity. She lost the opportunity to continue to enjoy her home, love her family and friends, and experience the good and not-so-good times life serves up to all of us. At age 36 she was dead—forever.

A jury is the most powerful institution in our justice system. Jury members are sworn to pass judgment based solely on the facts presented in a courtroom, without outside influence. If a jury arrives at a verdict under any other circumstances, the American justice system is harmed.

This system does have shortcomings. Some people can't handle the power a seat in the jury box gives them. They make critical decisions based on long-held bias instead of the facts of the case. Overconfidence bordering on arrogance can cause them to over-intellectualize the trial proceedings and to consider their reasoning skills flawless. These shortcomings can jeopardize the defendant's chances of getting a fair trial.

Racial, economic, and social prejudices are deeply set in the human psyche. A defendant's standing in the community may unfairly influence jury verdicts. Important people like doctors, sports heroes, revered clergymen, bankers, or wealthy business owners might receive a less harsh ruling because jurors admire them. Poor people who have no power or influence, especially those who have run afoul of the law in the past, in many cases are judged much harsher by biased jury members. Every defendant, innocent until proven guilty, has the right to be heard before an impartial court and to have legal counsel that will mount a forceful defense.

For those who don't know the Gilmore story, this book

gives them the chance to sit in a virtual juror's seat and judge Doctor Gilmore's innocence or guilt—absent of any improper influence that has become ever more prevalent in these types of celebrity cases.

Rule him innocent based on the facts in this mysterious case, not because he was a well loved, respected, and committed doctor. Find him guilty based on the evidence, not because he was a heavy drinker and perhaps harbored jealousy over his beautiful, much-younger wife who was flirtatious and could exhibit out-of-control behavior.

Prosecutors and defense lawyers manipulate prejudices when questioning potential jurors. A male sexist who thinks beautiful women are incapable of committing a crime will be a favorite choice of a defense lawyer with an attractive female client. Prosecutors will usually select candidates who believe criminals aren't punished severely enough. A critical responsibility of the presiding judge is to recognize the prejudices that always exist in every jury, to rule fairly and objectively, and to use his instructions to the panel to remind them to be objective and impartial.

The 1995 televised courtroom trial of ex-NFL football star O. J. Simpson for the murders of his ex-wife Nicole Brown Simpson and Ronald Goldman lasted over four months. The public became obsessed with the real-life drama. Based on the evidence, most people, even those who only casually followed the trial, were convinced Simpson would be convicted. When the verdict of "Not Guilty" was read before a national TV audience everyone was stunned, supporters and detractors alike. It was obvious by the expression on his face that O.J. was the most shocked person in the courtroom.

To further fan the flames of this example of outrageous jury malpractice, a juror replied to a question about the verdict, "We think he probably did it. We just didn't think they proved it beyond a reasonable doubt." That answer further offended the dignity and memory of the murdered victims. Many observers were convinced the disgraceful jury had made up their minds before the trial began. Simpson was later found guilty by a civil jury and assessed a large settlement in favor of the victims' families.

We Americans, including O. J. Simpson, are constitutionally guaranteed to be judged by our peers. No more handcuffs for him—O.J. walked away free. Ultimately he was sentenced to prison for unrelated theft offenses.

Another celebrity accused of killing his wife was former child movie star Robert Blake, who had later starred in the television detective show *Baretta*.

On May 4, 2001, Blake and his wife, Bonnie Lee Bakley, went to Vitello's Restaurant on Tujunga Avenue in Studio City, California. After dinner, Bakley was killed by a gunshot to the head while waiting in their car. Blake told police that he had gone back inside the restaurant to get a gun he had left at the table, and that he was there in the restaurant when the shooting took place. Blake's gun, a .38 caliber pistol, was tested and found not to be the gun that killed Bakley, which was later determined to be a 9 mm pistol. Witnesses remembered Blake returning to the restaurant at the same time he claimed his wife had been shot. Nobody testified having seen him return prior to that to retrieve the gun he said he left at the table where he and Bakley had dined.

Many are convinced that Blake killed Bakley, who was his second wife. They pointed out that Blake—he was her tenth husband—allegedly had tried to hire someone to kill her.

A jury, despite overwhelming evidence of his guilt, found him not guilty of murder and conspiracy to commit murder. Los Angeles district attorney Steve Cooley, when asked to comment on the jury's verdict, called Blake a "miserable human being" and the jurors "incredibly stupid." Blake's attorney, M. Gerald Schwartzbach, and members of the jury responded that the prosecution had failed to prove its case.

Later Blake, like Simpson, was found guilty in a civil court; consequently he suffered only financially. Bakley's three children filed a civil suit, and in 2005 were awarded $30,000,000 for the wrongful death of their mother. Blake filed for bankruptcy, listing debts of $3,000,000 in unpaid legal fees and tax liens.

Miscarriages of justice are not a recent development. An embedded part of American history is the nineteenth-century story of the infamous Lizzie Borden, who axed her parents to death. Perhaps it's appropriate to describe her jury as equally infamous—considering that they found her not guilty despite prosecution evidence that most modern legal scholars find compelling. The Bordens received 29 whacks with the axe, not the 81 suggested by the familiar folklore that has stuck around for years, a testament to the public's obsession with her 1893 murder trial. The unimaginably brutal nature of the crime was an obvious cause of the fixation; the fact that the defendant was the young daughter of the victims made the not guilty verdict even more shocking. It's hard for most people to imagine what a human's body looks like after being butchered to that extent by an axe. The jury spoke, and young and pretty Lizzie walked free.

In a case where a jury turned the tables, this one convicted Doctor Sam Sheppard of killing his pregnant 31-year-old wife

Marilyn in 1954. That famous murder trial inspired the hit TV series and film *The Fugitive*.

The Sheppard jury was bombarded with overwhelming media coverage that featured the details of the murder and the subsequent trial. Evidently the jurors were unable to meet the responsibilities to focus on the evidence and testimony—they succumbed to the tabloid smears, believing some or all of it. Doctor Sheppard walked to jail in chains.

In fairness to the Sheppard jury, DNA tests and other new genetic-testing methods have only recently provided evidence that blood found on Doctor Sheppard's pants and in his home was not his or his wife's, strongly indicating that an intruder could have bludgeoned Marilyn to death. Eventually, soon-to-become-famous lawyer F. Lee Bailey was hired to appeal to the federal courts that Sheppard did not receive a fair trial. Bailey filed a habeas corpus petition and was able to get Sheppard out of jail after ten years of confinement.

The federal court said that Sheppard's original trial "fell below the minimum requirements for due process." One of the judges of the court called Doctor Sheppard's original trial a "mockery of justice." Prosecutors didn't give up, however—they had Sheppard's original appeal overturned, although he was allowed to remain free, pending resolution of the matter. Eventually the U.S. Supreme Court agreed to examine the freedom of the press versus a defendant's right to a fair trial. The highest court in the land ruled 8–1 that although freedom of the press must be given due consideration, both criminal and civil matters are to be carried out in an objective, calm, and solemn courtroom setting. Doctor Sheppard died in 1970. The Sheppards' son, Sam Reese Sheppard, continues the battle to clear his father's name.

In 2008 Casey Anthony was charged with murdering her six-year-old daughter Caylee. The debacle that became the Casey Anthony trial with its high TV ratings became an entertainment event and bonanza for the press, drawing extraordinary coverage in national, international, and social media. Anthony's defense team protested that she was being tried in the media—it was a textbook example of unjust pretrial publicity that damaged the rights of their defendant.

Caylee Anthony was reported missing on July 15, 2008. Casey Anthony was charged with first-degree murder and pleaded not guilty in October 2008. Caylee's remains were found near the family home in December 2008.

The trial lasted six weeks, with the prosecutors seeking the death penalty. On July 5, 2011, the jury found Casey Anthony not guilty of murder, child abuse, and manslaughter of a child, but guilty of the minor offense of providing false information to police. It was another shocking verdict by a jury who many say lacked the ability, as a whole, to use rational judgment. Former Simpson trial prosecutor Marcia Clark stated that this jury confused reasonable doubt with reason to doubt Casey. Casey Anthony walked free.

If you decide, while reading this book, to become a virtual juror, you're obviously going to agree or disagree with the verdict that was handed down in 1987 by the actual Gilmore jury. You'll want to correct any mistakes you think the real-life participators made, and you'll want to solve the unknown, the unanswered, and the undiscovered circumstances that dominated this complicated case.

If you become one of the few who put all the components of the case to rest in your mind, it still won't change reality. The case remains a mystery, and even though much of the memory and the speculation about it will fade away, as history always does, it will long continue to be an open case in the minds of many.

Fortunately, understanding and interpreting all the evidence in the long series of events allows the reader the luxury of judging Doctor Gilmore's innocence or guilt without the stress of being a member of yet another improperly influenced jury.

Patricia Gilmore's tragic death marked the beginning of a long, tangled web of legal proceedings that matched a determined team of prosecutors against a shrewd and well-respected defense attorney.

Introduction

Patricia Ann Wolfe was a child of the 1960s. Called Patty, she was born in 1944, about two years too old to technically be a "baby boomer," but she nevertheless was born as a result of the social revolution that occurred after World War II when America had to make room for all the young men who fought hard and now wanted to have a wife, kids, a house, a television, and at least one car in the driveway.

She was born and raised in Muhlenberg, an area located a hundred miles or so northwest of Philadelphia. Muhlenberg is a suburb just north of and abutting the city of Reading, Pennsylvania. Small communities within Muhlenberg include the towns of Temple and Laureldale.

Her mother, Molly (Beane) Wolfe, died when Patty was young. Her father, Irvin Wolfe, had a reputation for being stubborn—it was his way or no way. He was possessive and protective of Patty, a trait many widowers might take with a young daughter. Patty was close to her father; she loved and respected him all her life. When Irvin remarried, Patty found herself surrounded, in addition to her stepmother Julia, with a half brother, a stepbrother, and a stepsister.

Starting school in 1950, she seemed to do well as a kid growing up in the fast-changing times during the 1950s. By the end of the decade this class of 1962 had founded rock n' roll with the advent of Buddy Holly, Richie Valens, Chuck Berry, and of course Elvis Presley. As the class entered junior high school in 1957 these kids got interested in dancing, so school dances became the springboard for an almost obsession with music, music that was pioneering and fast changing. While they moved on and grew through the slinky, silly putty, frisbee, poodle skirt, and hula hoop phases, they raced home from school every day to watch the Philadelphia-based TV show *American Bandstand*. The kids at Muhlenberg High School copied the Philly kids' dances, fashion style, and dating and courtship rituals such as *going steady* and *breaking up*. The music was offensive to many adults because it was performed by both black and white entertainers, becoming a mix of the blues and country music, the recipe that made rock n' roll the biggest item of social revolution in twentieth-century America.

It was a decade of unprecedented economic and population growth. The high birthrate lowered the average age. By 1958 one-third of the population of America was younger than fifteen years old. The baby boom had begun in the years following World War II. From 1948 to 1953 more children were born than in the previous thirty years. 1954 saw America experience the largest one-year population increase ever. Some worried about over population, but were reminded that each new person would become another consumer to help expand and support the economy.

It was America's first decade as a world superpower. School kids crawled under their desks during drills reacting to a mock nuclear attack. They were taught that the Soviet Union and Communist China were determined to destroy America.

The baby boom was in full speed ahead. As the 1950s closed and the 1960s appeared, members of this class of 1962 saw John Kennedy as a leader that inspired them, and they began paying attention to issues such as civil rights and women's rights; and, with America's involvement in southeast Asia, many became activists, marching in protest.

Muhlenberg High School was a pleasant oasis from much of

the stress that many youth in other areas of America had to deal with. Located in affluent Laureldale with its tree-lined streets and meticulously cared-for homes, it provided a sheltered environment. The Muhlenberg School District includes Temple and Laureldale; plus Hyde Park, Muhlenberg Park, Riverview Park, and other communities within the Muhlenberg area.

Many years earlier, in 1737, the first European settlers, mostly of German and English descent, began to occupy and settle parts of Muhlenberg and the surrounding communities. Named after Henry Augustus Muhlenberg, a member of one of the more prominent and influential families of Berks County, Muhlenberg began to change from a strictly farming community when in 1914 Rosedale Knitting Mills began operating in Laureldale as a manufacturer of men's and women's stockings. By 1921, Rosedale employed nearly 3,000 persons—many settled close to the site of operations. Laureldale was officially incorporated in 1930. The name "Laureldale" was selected since "Rosedale" was already an existing community in Chester County. The mill eventually ceased operations in 1952.

The village of Temple was established in 1853, named after a hotel and restaurant on the town square known as "Solomon's Temple." Temple was officially incorporated as a town in 1922. Beginning about 1935, Italian immigrants began a prosperous mushroom growing and processing industry, which put Temple on the map as a prominent agricultural community specializing in mushrooms.

The old high school was still being used, but a brand new junior high school awaited the class of 1962 when they started seventh grade. It was a new design for the East: kids walking outside between classes on covered walkways between buildings during all types of weather, including rain, snow, and freezing temperatures—without any boots, coats, or even sweaters. The school directors were criticized for creating such an albatross. It looked new and it smelled new, but it lacked practicality for a region with changing seasons. It didn't have the tradition and atmosphere of the high school.

When it was time to move up to the old and historic high school, the class members discovered an appreciation of tradition as they walked the hallways of the 1930s building, It had spirit: school spirit.

Patty was arguably the prettiest girl in her class, culminating in being a member of the May Queen Court. She grew up to become a woman with an unusual and overwhelming beauty, pure and natural.

After two previous marriages, Patty became a doctor's wife. The Gilmores were married in June 1970. Being a doctor's wife was the main ingredient for her now wonderful life; she had status and money. Better yet was being married to a very popular small-town doctor who couldn't go anywhere without some person calling out "Hi, Doc." The love and respect that people had for her husband, whether they were patients of his or not, cascaded down over her and gave her the opportunity to become a leader in the community. She got appointed as a board member of the local American Heart Association and the American Red Cross, and was a member of the Junior League and the Young Republicans Club.

Gilmore worshipped the ground that Patty walked on. He was commonly known by everyone as *Doc* but her favorite nickname for him was *Gilly*. He bought her everything she asked for; he could afford it. They both drove late-model Cadillacs.

Their home at 4100 Kutztown Road in South Temple was a handsome and stately two-story brick home just a mile from the bungalow at 5313 Allentown Boulevard, on the north edge of Temple, that housed his office.

She had a cedar closet on the third floor that contained her many fur and leopard-skin coats. After the local women snubbed her at the South Temple Swimming Pool, she got him to install her own in-ground pool in their backyard, complete with a pool house and privacy fencing.

The house had an extensive alarm system wired direct to the Muhlenberg Police Department. When Patty was drunk or in a pestering mood, she would intentionally set off the alarm and make him get out of bed to reset it while the cops were on their way.

The police didn't mind: he was the local doctor as well as a deputy coroner who always supported them while they performed their duties. Gilmore made house calls long after most doctors, even general practitioners like him, stopped. Patrolmen on duty would happen upon his Cadillac sitting in front of a house with the driver's door wide open and the motor running, obviously responding to an urgent call. The police officer sat in the patrol car dutifully guarding the car until medical care was dispensed.

Detective Barry Hadley and Gilmore eventually became adversaries, but back in June of 1975 a large Afghan stray dog had attacked then Muhlenberg Patrolman Hadley. Hadley had responded to the stray dog report and when he approached the dog it knocked him down to the sidewalk and bit him on the face, right arm, and left leg. Hadley shot the dog in the head during the attack. Gilmore treated him for his wounds. John DiGiamberardino, the owner of the dog, and ironically one of the Gilmores' neighbors, stated that the dog's collar broke.

According to sources, one of Patty's favorite drinking companions was the wife of a successful restaurant owner. When they were both too drunk to drive her Cadillac home, she'd call the Muhlenberg Police and the closest patrolman would come and pick her up and take her home, or she'd ask them to call her husband and have him come to get them.

There were alleged affairs. Supposedly Gilmore knew about them. It was said he also had his share of indiscretions. As long as Patty came home to him he seemed content. She evidently learned that being a doctor's wife requires sacrifices, primarily periods of loneliness because of the long hours he worked. She learned to adjust to that negative part of their relationship, although reportedly she did complain to her neighbor that he seemed to be more committed to his patients than to her.

Evidently that loneliness and resulting boredom prompted her to get a job as a tipstaff at the Berks County Courthouse. That position is closely related to the duties performed by a bailiff in most jurisdictions—maintaining decorum in the courtroom. Tipstaff personnel in Berks County don't wear uniforms; a fact that allowed Patty to wear her expensive dresses while carrying out her duties. She seemed to be doing well.

Irvin Gilmore was born in Picture Rocks, Lycoming County, Pennsylvania, son of the late Irvin and Mary (Sterner) Gilmore. He was a graduate of Hughesville High School, Lehigh University, Bethlehem, Pennsylvania, and Jefferson Medical School, Philadelphia. A Navy veteran of World War II, Gilmore served as a deacon of his church.

Gilmore grew attached to the area and decided to settle down in Muhlenberg while serving as a resident intern at the Reading Hospital. He became quite active in charitable activities. News articles reported his participating in the hospital's 1952 Garden Party, held on the hospital's south lawn by the

women volunteers. The women, members of the various aux-
iliaries, church groups, and social clubs, raised money to buy
necessary linens and much- needed equipment for the hospital,
and funded scholarships for student nurses. These volunteers
performed over 10,000 volunteer hours during that year, offering direct service to patients, sewing and folding bandages,
distributing flowers, books, and magazines, washing dishes,
working at the gift shop, and waiting on tables in the snack bar.
Gilmore supported and participated in these types of events.

He began his lucrative practice in the Temple bungalow
in September 1952, and served his patients until he retired in
1990. News reports at the time announcing the new practice
listed Mrs. Gilmore as the former Betty Crawley, with their
son Barry, age nine months. His medical practice continuous-
ly grew over the years, mostly because of his attentiveness to
his patients and his caring and nurturing method of providing
medical care to the many families that relied on him. Because
he had a warm, sincere personality, his extensive list of friends
also kept expanding. He continued to work hard, seeing patients during morning hours, evening hours, and many times
house calls during the middle of the night.

Later he was named a deputy coroner of Berks County,
which allowed him to assist the local police when investigating a natural or accidental death. The next month after he had
treated Officer Hadley for dog bites, he was summoned by
police to, acting as a deputy coroner, pronounce two young
men dead after they were murdered by a mushroom-growing
plant worker and his son. Gilmore ordered autopsies to be performed which confirmed the findings that the men died from
chest wounds. In May of 1978 he completed continuing-educa-
tion requirements to retain active membership in the American

Academy of Family Physicians, formerly called the American Academy of General Practice.

When he wasn't working they partied hard and drank hard. That's when being a doctor's wife, and being a doctor married to a young beautiful woman made it all seem worth it. The hard-working doctor always had an active social life. He liked good food, good drink, and having a good time. He liked to take Patty to Stokesay Castle, a fine-dining restaurant featuring Tudor architecture located on Mt. Penn overlooking the city of Reading. There were other hangouts; their favorite apparently was the Whit-Mar Inn, where they regularly drank and dined. The restored eighteenth-century building with thick walls of limestone was originally known as the Gehret Mansion that became established as a local stagecoach stop in 1854. The place was later known successively as Poor Richard's Tavern, the Apple Inn, Lesher's Hotel, and finally the Whit-Mar Inn. It was located in the western part of Muhlenberg about 3 miles from the Gilmore's house. It was demolished in 1999 to make room for a convenience store.

Typical of Pennsylvania German folklore, the Whit-Mar Inn was branded as haunted. The ghosts of an old woman and an Indian had been spotted peering from the windows. The old lady's ghost would slam doors shut, turn the lights off and on, along with the air conditioner at times. Some have claimed to see the ghostly figure of an Indian in the back of the building.

Doctor Gilmore's drink of choice was martinis while Patty liked Dewar's White Label Scotch. They typically would have two drinks at the bar before eating dinner. After dinner they would talk with friends and drink some more, and then somehow make it home.

Gilmore appeared on the society pages before and after his

marriage to Patty. A July 1958 news item told of Doctor Irvin Gilmore and Mrs. Betty Gilmore having dinner as invited guests of Bob Hope's famed bandleader Les Brown at the Hershey Hotel in Hershey, Pennsylvania. They attended many dinner parties and open houses hosted by influential people and their spouses, and held many themselves.

The 1962 Amethyst Ball, held at the Berkshire Country Club in Reading, sponsored by the Staff Doctors' Wives of the Reading Hospital, was reported in the press as a major social event. Cocktail parties preceded the ball, and the Gilmore party was held at 3300 Willow Grove Avenue, in Muhlenberg Park, his residence at the time with his wife Betty. According to news reports, noted patron of the arts Gertrude Sternbergh and professional baseball player Rocky Colavito and his wife were Gilmore guests. The news article even described Betty Gilmore's gown as floor length of turquoise chiffon, décolleté, and a stole of the same material, folded gracefully backward and reaching the floor.

The surprise fiftieth birthday party in 1972 that Patty, the new Mrs. Gilmore, threw for her husband at the Berkshire Country Club received news coverage, just two months after they returned from a trip to Paris.

There is no doubt that being a medical doctor requires enduring stress from being forced to cope with long hours and constant exposure to sickness and injury. An-often used mode of release is the abuse of alcohol and drugs. The Gilmores drank, especially Patty. She never suffered the effects of long-term alcohol abuse; she didn't live long enough.

The Gilmores were casual friends with most of the regular patrons of the Whit-Mar Inn, including the owner Harry Kore, who also worked as bartender. Kore had a two-martini limit on Gilmore. Patty and Gilmore came to the Whit-Mar Inn for dinner, never just to drink. Frequently Patty would sit at the bar talking to people while Gilmore would have dinner.

Gilmore and Patty also liked attending dinner parties at friends' homes. It was Thanksgiving morning 1980, the morning after attending one of those get-togethers, that the tragic end to Patty Gilmore's life occurred.

People who paid attention to the death of Patty, and the subsequent prosecution of Gilmore for her murder, typically relied on condensed news-media coverage of the tragedy to formulate their opinions about the crime—if in fact there was a crime. Devotion to, and yes in some cases contempt toward, a beloved leader of the community, the family doctor, caused high emotions to be factored in. Rumors, innuendoes, falsehoods, and speculation based on ignorance ran rampant at the time, and many of these factors still exist today.

Chapter
1

Death at the
Gilmore House

It would be years later that Doctor Irvin Gilmore would be put on trial for criminal homicide. Facts and rumors prevailed and would get mixed up long after Patrolman Thomas Dougherty of the Muhlenberg Police Department entered the Gilmore residence that Thanksgiving morning, November 27, 1980, and failed to recognize the house as a possible crime scene. His job on that gloomy day with overcast clouds, drizzling rain, and a chilly 35 F degrees, was to routinely patrol the affluent villages of the Muhlenberg area and make sure plenty of peaceful quiet was maintained for the traditional family holiday. His patrolling turned out to be far from routine. He happened upon a situation he was not prepared for, and because of that did not follow basic police protocol—he compromised the possible crime scene by traipsing around and handling potential evidence. Most importantly however, he failed to request experienced crime investigators to come to Doctor Gilmore's home immediately.

Around 8 a.m. Dougherty overheard on his radio a dispatch call that the Muhlenberg Ambulance was responding to the Gilmores' South Temple home. Dougherty was only a block and a half away from the Gilmore house when he monitored the emergency call. Dougherty, like all the Muhlenberg cops and other emergency workers, knew Doctor Gilmore, and he immediately recognized the address. Gilmore had given Dougherty his physical when he was hired, and treated him for colds and other minor ailments; and Dougherty also had known Patty for about three years—since he became a member of the Muhlenberg Police Force.

Dougherty later testified that he drove the block and a half to see if he could be of any assistance. He was northbound when he arrived at the location, pulling up on the wrong side of the street so that the driver's side of the patrol car was against the curb in front of the house. He recalled that a young man, who identified himself as Barry Gilmore, Doctor Gilmore's son, met him at the curb, asked him to hurry up, and told him that he believes Patty Gilmore was dead. Officer Dougherty entered the house and went upstairs to the second floor bedroom where Doctor Gilmore was. Patty was lying on the bed.

Dougherty was now already in over his head. He failed to realize that he could possibly be in the midst of a crime scene, that he should make sure that nothing was disturbed, and that he should place a call to his superior officer before allowing the body to be moved. Muhlenberg Police would then have had the option of doing a preliminary on-site investigation and contacting the Berks County District Attorney's office if they felt it was warranted.

According to Dougherty's testimony given at the Gilmore preliminary hearing the following year on July 29, 1981, he stated that when he entered the bedroom Patricia Gilmore was lying on the left side of the bed on her back. He immediately went over to her and felt her neck to see if he could feel a pulse. He recalled that the neck was very stiff, there was no pulse, and the body was very cold. He noted that Doctor Gilmore was on the right side of the bed on the telephone. He said he didn't know whom Doctor Gilmore was talking to, nor did he overhear any of the conversation. Despite the room being poorly lit, he noticed that the body had a grayish tint to it and he didn't notice any bruises, marks, or cuts—no contusions on her face. Dougherty would also testify that he didn't see any contusions on her face after he observed it later at the Reading Hospital. He did, however, notice several needle marks on her right buttock. Dougherty testified that Doctor George Kershner, a member of the hospital staff, pointed out the marks to him.

When the ambulance arrived, Dougherty got Doctor Gilmore to go downstairs and into the kitchen because he didn't want him to watch the ambulance personnel remove his wife's body.

Lucille Genslinger, driver and attendant for the Muhlenberg Ambulance Association, was on duty that Thanksgiving Day from 6 a.m. until twelve noon. She responded, with two other crew members, to a call at the Gilmore residence at 9 a.m. Barry Gilmore greeted Genslinger and her crew and escorted them to the second-floor bedroom.

Genslinger testified that she found Patty lying on her back and checked her carotid artery for a pulse; she failed to find one. While her two attendants went downstairs to get the equipment needed, she remained upstairs and stayed in the bedroom. She recalled that the body was cold and blue, and rigor mortis was starting to set in, and she noted that no body secretions or fluids were on the bed or the body. She testified that she did not see any bruises or contusions on Patty's face.

Dougherty later recalled that Doctor Gilmore was highly upset, crying, and walking around in a daze, a state of shock. While he sat in the kitchen with Doctor Gilmore, Dougherty began his own police investigation instead of calling for experienced help. He observed the kitchen, typical in almost every way. Gilmore said Patty was preparing dog food for the dog. It was sitting on the counter. There were pots, pans, and bottles on the counter and in the sink.

Dougherty asked Gilmore when was the last time he saw his wife alive, and if she was depressed or on any kind of medication. The doctor said that he didn't think his wife was taking any medication, and that he hadn't noticed any signs of depression. He said that he had gone to bed early the night before, leaving Patty and his daughter-in-law Linda Gilmore sitting in the kitchen, where they talked until about 2 a.m. when Linda went to bed.

After finishing his questioning, Dougherty conducted a preliminary search of the house, particularly the room where Patty was located. The officer observed nothing out of the ordinary in that room or any of the other rooms upstairs located on both sides of a center hallway, but Gilmore's son, Barry, mentioned that he believed a syringe was missing from the doctor's bag. The medical bag was located in a front room, used as a study, on the left side of the hallway adjacent to the Gilmores' bedroom. On the right side of the hall, across from the bedroom, was a back room with attached bathroom that Patty used for a dressing room. Barry Gilmore showed Dougherty the bag, but the officer never asked Barry or Doctor Gilmore if the bag was moved into the room before he arrived, or if that's where they found the bag in the morning. No inventory of the bag's contents was taken, although a chrome instrument—possibly an empty syringe protector—and vials of medication were observed.

It was in the dressing room where he found the syringe. Dougherty testified that he found it on a table across from a dressing chair, a lounge-type chair. He stated that there wasn't any needle in the syringe, and that he looked for the needle all over the upstairs of the house but failed to find it.

In what surely was a serious breach of basic police work, Dougherty kept the syringe in his possession, after finding a small amount of a brown-colored liquid in it, until he personally carried it to the Pennsylvania State Police Laboratory in Bethlehem, Pennsylvania.

When Dougherty picked up the syringe, Gilmore or Barry reportedly commented that Dougherty should be careful with it in case of fingerprints, and that his response was that it wasn't necessary because it was obviously a suicide. Later Dougherty denied having said that when he testified at the Gilmore preliminary hearing on July 29, 1981, eight months after Patty's death. Questioned further by defense counsel, he was asked if it is possible that he made the comment and simply didn't remember it. Dougherty responded, "All I can say is I don't recall making it."

Dougherty testified that he didn't see any contusions on Patty Gilmore's face after he observed her body at the Reading Hospital, only the needle marks on her right buttock that Doctor Kershner had pointed out to him.

In Dougherty's official report, he used the terminology "upper right thigh, the rump cheek" in describing the location of the marks. When asked later by defense counsel what he meant by that he said he meant the marks were above her thigh but below her waist. He confirmed at that time that the marks were on the buttock, and that they were in fact needle marks.

Dougherty stated that it was he who had raised the question of an autopsy, but he didn't talk directly with the coroner's office. Instead he asked Doctor Kershner to tell the coroner's office that he requests that an autopsy be done. He also informed Kershner that when the autopsy is scheduled he was to contact the Muhlenberg Police and that somebody from their office would be present.

Officer Dougherty had arrived at the Gilmore house at approximately 9:02 a.m. He spent just a short time there; after about twenty or twenty-five minutes he was on his way to the Reading Hospital, where he met with Kershner and the Muhlenberg Ambulance attendants.

Prosecutors had questioned Genslinger why her crew didn't try to render any assistance to Patty Gilmore. She testified that due to the condition of the body, and with Doctor Gilmore present, she felt if the body could have been resuscitated, it probably would have been tried before the ambulance's arrival. What turned out to be a very important element of the impending legal case was the possible bruising of the body during this transport, and of course once the body arrived at the hospital.

The body, dressed in a nightshirt and bikini underpants, was placed on a very heavy canvas-type litter, which is flexible and more convenient for ambulance personnel to carry people downstairs. Once downstairs, the body and canvas litter were placed right on the ambulance litter. The body was secured with three straps on the canvas litter and three straps on the ambulance litter itself. In addition the ambulance litter is secured by a bar that runs alongside the ambulance and is locked in.

Genslinger testified that she rode in the back of the ambulance with the body during the ride to Reading Hospital, that the face was not covered during the trip, giving her more opportunity to confirm the lack of any bruises or contusions. Genslinger stated that she did not at any time observe the body being bumped or bruised in any way, or that anything hit the body, and that the body did not bump or touch the sides of the ambulance. Genslinger confirmed that she did not see anything come in contact with the body at all.

At the hospital the body was turned over to Doctor Kershner, who, as Officer Dougherty had already found out, was the doctor on duty. Genslinger knew Kershner by sight and by name. The body was then transferred from the ambulance litter to the hospital litter. Genslinger testified that she did not see the body strike any object or any object strike the body while it was being turned over to Kershner.

Chapter
2

The Interrogation

Doctor Gilmore voluntarily appeared at the Berks County Courthouse in Reading on December 11, 1980, to give a sworn oral statement that Muhlenberg Police Chief Harley Smith intended to use to spearhead a murder investigation that his department was clearly not qualified to define or conduct. The first indication that the small-town department, consisting of about fifteen persons, was in over its head was Patrolman Thomas P. Dougherty's failure to recognize—and as a result compromising—a possible crime scene when he had arrived at the Gilmore home Thanksgiving morning.

Doctor Gilmore, cocksure and confident that he wasn't a crime suspect, prepared to cooperate with the authorities. Because he was a physician, he was able to turn the tables on his questioners by imparting medical fact and opinion not privy to them, thus enabling him to retain a certain amount of control of the interrogation. He was being questioned, without legal counsel, about the circumstances of his wife's death that already began to appear quite complex, so complex that fact-finding would pose a challenge to even well-qualified and seasoned crime investigators.

Selected to question Gilmore in addition to Chief Smith were Detective Barry Hadley and Detective Sergeant Kermit Frantz, all of the Muhlenberg Police Department, and Stuart Suss, Berks County assistant district attorney.

Smith gave Gilmore the necessary Miranda warnings, asking him if he understood his rights and if he was willing to give a statement, which Gilmore acknowledged.

Smith, who according to reliable sources had come to believe that Gilmore was guilty of first-degree murder, led off the questioning

CHIEF SMITH: Okay, okay, Doctor. We are all aware of the tragic death of your wife. As I say, we are not here to exaggerate anything, but up until yesterday we had no final report from the pathology lab at the Reading Hospital as to what exactly had taken place, although we had conferred with both Doctor Keith and Doctor Neal Hoffman of the pathology lab at the Reading Hospital.

DOCTOR GILMORE: Yes.

CHIEF SMITH: Doctor Keith performed the autopsy. I think that was on the—

DOCTOR GILMORE: It was the same day as her death.

CHIEF SMITH: Yes. It was Thanksgiving eve or Thanksgiving evening. There were some toxicology that wasn't done at the Reading Hospital. They had that done at the Upjohn Lab, and results were just sent back. That, along with some other problems— we didn't have a report from the coroner's office. Doctor Glosser was out of town. He went to Mexico. Doctor Myers gave Detective Hadley a probable cause of the death which wasn't consistent with the pathology report. After reviewing this with both Doctor Keith and Doctor Hoffman, we felt that there was—

DOCTOR GILMORE: I understand.

CHIEF SMITH: —some things we had to clear up, and the only way to do this was to speak to you,—

DOCTOR GILMORE: Uh-huh.

CHIEF SMITH: So would you mind starting perhaps from the night before and, you know, giving us a statement as to what had transpired and who you were with up until the time you discovered your wife dead.

DOCTOR GILMORE: Certainly. I would like to start the night before that. The night before that my wife gave a course in CPR down at Stony Creek Mills. She failed to show at a time that I thought was correct, so that I was up prancing around. She was supposed to be home at 11:30. She got home at 3:00, but she had developed cable trouble with her battery. I'm saying this because I was unable to sleep the rest of the night.

"In any case, the next day my son arrived. I thought—what I am telling you now I did not think until I got the report from you today. She told me in the kitchen just before she was going to pick up my son that she had had diarrhea for nine days, and I said, 'Well, what are you taking?' She said she was taking Lomotil, l-o-m-o-t—can't even spell it. L-o-m-o-t-i-l. I said, well, if it isn't helping, why not try Imodium, because she had taken some drug on and off for diarrhea. She sort of had an irritable cold and it sort of fluctuated between constipation and diarrhea, and I think she was sort of excited by my son and his wife coming. I said, 'Why don't you try Imodium?' She responded, 'I'll stay with the Lomotil. It's worked for me before.'

"She went to pick up my son and his wife, came back to our home. We went to the home of Mr. And Mrs. Mathew Amoroso for dinner. We had several cocktails. My wife, I think, had some scotch. We had a typically Italian meal of spaghetti, meatballs and red wine, which my wife does not really handle that well with regard to nausea and vomiting. In fact, on many occasions on drinking wine of any amount at all—and she did do this quite frequently because she belonged to, as you know, the Junior League. She would come home from meetings and would be suffering pretty—almost always, at least, before I would go to the office in the morning headache, nausea, vomiting. I was very leery about giving her any type of medication until I found a drug Stadol, S-t-a-d-o-l, which is a non-narcotic pain depressant which took away her headaches.

"We came home from Amorosos', I would say, roughly around 12:30. My wife drove home. I was—I had several drinks, but they did nothing to me except make me more sleepy, so I excused myself and went to bed. My wife—my son's wife stayed up and talked to her until around 2:00 when she came to bed.

"My neighbors, Mr. And Mrs. John D. DiGiamberardino, heard her go out to the car and talk to the dog, and then she came in. In retrospect, I'm sure this is when she went out and got my bag, which is nothing new, come, wake me up and I'd give her a shot of Stadol. Okay. I, however, am not that heavy a sleeper. I was not awakened at night.

"I woke up in the morning. My wife was lying next to me. I went to the bathroom. I came back to bed and I noticed that she seemed awfully cold. I reached—I reached over to pull more blankets over her, although she seemed adequately covered, and I discovered she was awfully cold. I turned her over, and she was obviously dead.

"I don't know what I did then except I jumped out of bed and I called my son and his wife. I saw my bag in the dressing room, which is across the hall from my own. I immediately went through it. I could not find a two cc syringe. I'm told that an officer found it later on top of a radio that's in her room. I went through—I went through the bag immediately. There was a bottle of Demerol, which I'm sure I had acquired maybe two or three days before because I was running out. I would like to add here that my wife could not take Demerol. She got very sick on it. She was told by Doctor Menges who had operated on her foot that, you know, Demerol was a no-no for her. It's a stupid drug, anyhow. I still use it primarily to treat migraine headaches. He said if she ever has it and, as a matter of fact, during that illness—she had both feet operated on—I did give her occasionally a shot of M.S. [morphine sulfate?], but this is several years ago.

"In any case, I went through my bag. The—the Demerol bottle that I had was new. One cc was missing, and I'm sure to my recollection of one of my nurses giving that to a patient in the office. Demerol was out of my head. It wouldn't have been in my head, anyhow. I looked in at the Stadol. There didn't seem to be any Stadol missing, but I'm not sure. I looked at the morphine. The morphine I had ordered because I was almost out of it. There was perhaps not even a full dose left in it the day before. The same amount was there at that time.

"Several days later in an ashtray I found a bent needle. I went looking for it principally because I was told by the pathologist that she had needle marks on her buttock, and I really—I really felt scared because I felt that it was possible that she had come to my bedroom possibly after trying to give herself a shot of Stadol and that I might have given her a shot and that it might have contributed to her death. I don't think that's possible because I have—never mind. I have never poked anyone five times with a needle. This was a two cc syringe. I awaited—the report.

"Now, the death certificate said she died from asphyxiation from probably inhaling or swallowing vomit. This did not make sense to me because how can someone aspirate laying next to you in bed without one hell of a—a to-do. I thought she had probably died of what we call cardiac arrest or electrical death. I wanted to think that. I talked to Doctor Irving Imber about it and he said it was quite possible. I still, however, wondered about the Stadol, but—and I was being self-accusatory because I felt, damn it, who could have given it? Then I decided after talking to Doctor Imber and went through all of this self-incrimination, even if I had given her every damn drop of Stadol, it wouldn't have been sufficient to cause respiratory suppression. Stadol is given even to people with head injuries. I don't know if you remember the accident on the Fifth Street Highway where the girl was pinned. She had head injuries, and that was a perfectly safe drug to give her.

"In any case, the doctor also told me a toxicology was going to be done. I said I would welcome it. I wanted to know if there was any Stadol in her. I got this report today and it said that she had five times as much or whatever to kill her, and then it struck. Remember when I said she said she had diarrhea for nine days and was taking Lomotil? If you care to read—if you care to read what Lomotil is, it's a combination of a meperidine-like drug and atropine, and it should be given no more that two or four times a day. It can cause respiratory suppression and it can act as—it can give you the side effects of not only atropine but Demerol.

"Okay. I had three of these [*indicating*]. Now, this one is—two are missing, but she had, I'm sure—these are samples that we had at the office. Okay. I am sure she had at least one of these in her room, although I can't—I cannot prove that because I wanted—wanted her clothing out and any of that—I'm almost positive, however, that she must have run out because David Pollock, a friend of mine from Buffalo, was with me—that's incorrect. My son was with me from the time of her death until Sunday last. Mrs. Pollock was with me until that time. David came down last weekend and asked if he might take some medication back, since he claims he doesn't trust any other doctor, which is pure poppycock, but I gave him some Naldecon, which is for a head cold, and I went to give him a full pack of these [*indicating*]. In other words, this much was gone [*indicating*] plus a whole one, which would be—well, it would be 3, 6, 9, 12, 14, 16, 18, 20, 22, 24.

MR. SUSS: Doctor, pardon me for interrupting, but because we are dealing with a printed record, can you describe a little more fully what it is you are holding in your hand?

DOCTOR GILMORE: Okay, I'm holding a sample package of Lomotil. I'm sorry. It's a thirty-pack tablet dispenser.

MR. SUSS: Can you specify exactly what was missing that you described from the packet?

DOCTOR GILMORE: Okay. These two [*indicating*] were missing.

MR. SUSS: You are talking about two end tablets from a thirty-tablet packet?

DOCTOR GILMORE: I'm talking about three end tablets. One whole packet was missing. In other words, there were three packets.

MR. SUSS: Three packets containing thirty tablets?

DOCTOR GILMORE: Right. Okay.

MR. SUSS: An entire packet of thirty—

DOCTOR GILMORE: Was missing.

MR. SUSS: —was missing.

DOCTOR GILMORE: I know that my wife had some in her own room.

MR. SUSS: Are you also saying that three more were missing from a second packet, three individual tablets?

DOCTOR GILMORE: No. I'm saying that the one I gave Mr. Pollock, fifteen were missing. Okay. Now then, my wife had a—a real anger when it came to not feeling better. I am almost positive – I would gladly—I am almost positive that, when she came to bed, she must have—I don't say that she did. I say she must have been taking more—Lomotil has about a thirty-hour life span in the body. If she would have taken four, six—I would much rather have you check the validity of this statement with the pathologist—I think it could have killed her. If you care to look at the PDR and look at overdose—I guest that's my statement. It's killed before

CHIEF SMITH: I'm sorry. Lomotil has killed before, you say?

DOCTOR GILMORE: Oh yes. You can have those tablets [*indicating*], incidentally.

DETECTIVE HADLEY: I don't think we need it.

CHIEF SMITH: All we need, Doctor, is—all right. Doctor, if I may ask you some questions —

DOCTOR GILMORE: Okay.

CHIEF SMITH: Have you seen the autopsy report?

DOCTOR GILMORE: No.

CHIEF SMITH: This is a copy of the official autopsy report.

DOCTOR GILMORE: Uh-huh.

CHIEF SMITH: There are some things here—we are not medical personnel, of course.

DOCTOR GILMORE: Okay.

CHIEF SMITH: Doctor Keith did explain some of the findings to us in layman's terms. Number one, you last saw your wife that evening approximately 1 a.m.—that would have been—

DOCTOR GILMORE: 12:30. She was in the kitchen.

CHIEF SMITH: It was early Thursday morning. Okay. She had been drinking.

DOCTOR GILMORE: Yes.

CHIEF SMITH: Okay.

DOCTOR GILMORE: I don't —I don't consider that she was bombed. She drove home, as I said, but she could drive. My wife could hold a fair amount of liquor and drive, but as soon as she got home, she was sick.

CHIEF SMITH: Okay. Had your wife fallen or sustained any injuries prior to you going out or during the evening?

DOCTOR GILMORE: No. I understand that she had a bruise on her cheek, but she would frequently fall if she would come upstairs. She had quite a few bruises from time to time, but I was told that she had a bruise on her cheek.

CHIEF SMITH: Okay. The report reveals she had a quite—in layman's terms, a severe bruise under the right eye.

Doctor Gilmore: That would be on the cheek.

Chief Smith: Yes. The right cheek under the right eye.

Doctor Gilmore: Yes. Uh-huh.

Chief Smith: In the autopsy it was hemorrhaged severely underneath.

Doctor Gilmore: Okay.

Chief Smith: She had a bruise on the left side of her nose.

Doctor Gilmore: [*moving head vertically*]

Chief Smith: She had a bruise that would cause hemorrhaging to the center part of her forehead.

Doctor Gilmore: Uh-huh.

Chief Smith: She also had a bruise—I'm saying "bruise." It was a—a—a hemorrhage was obvious in her scalp. It was to the rear of her head.

Doctor Gilmore: Yes.

Chief Smith: So, actually, she had four—

Doctor Gilmore: Bruises.

Chief Smith: —bruises or four hemorrhages or four areas— three areas that hemorrhaged and one that we can't really describe on the left side of her nose.

Doctor Gilmore: Okay.

Chief Smith: Would you have any idea how this type of injury occurred?

Doctor Gilmore: My wife frequently has fallen going out the back steps. If we are discussing head, it would have to have been an accidental fall, possibly coming up the steps. It depends. The steps are carpeted. I wouldn't see that heavy a thing. There is no carpeting on the steps that go out back of the house. I think—I think if she would have had a severe fall coming up the steps, my son and his wife would have heard it because their door was still open.

DETECTIVE HADLEY: Where were they sleeping at, Doctor?

DOCTOR GILMORE: They were sleeping in the guest room right across from our room.

DETECTIVE HADLEY: Up on the second floor?

DOCTOR GILMORE: Uh-huh.

CHIEF SMITH: Were these obvious to you the next morning, Doctor, when you—

DOCTOR GILMORE: Nothing was obvious to me.

CHIEF SMITH: I understand it was a trauma, but you didn't—

DOCTOR GILMORE: No. Her face was quite red and flattened where she had been sleeping on it. I saw no bruises, but I did not examine her for bruises.

CHIEF SMITH: Were you aware of the needle marks on her right buttocks?

DOCTOR GILMORE: Not until I was told by the pathologist.

CHIEF SMITH: According to the report, she had four to five needle marks in her right buttocks.

DOCTOR GILMORE: And he told me he was going to excise the skin and examine it for drugs.

CHIEF SMITH: Yes. That specimen has been taken and is in the possession of the pathology lab.

DOCTOR GILMORE: Uh-huh.

CHIEF SMITH: These were very recent. Would you have any idea how these were administered or this type—?

DOCTOR GILMORE: I have never—I have never known her to give herself a shot, but my son and wife were home. She might well have tried and not done too well. I would think the—I would think if they found any drug, however, it would be Stadol because I'm sure that's what she was trying to take. She would certainly not try to take Demerol.

CHIEF SMITH: The toxology results indicate she had a 0.24 blood alcohol reading.

DOCTOR GILMORE: Yes, I understand that.

CHIEF SMITH: Okay. Along with that they did drug screening. The only positive results were Demerol.

DOCTOR GILMORE: That's meperidine.

CHIEF SMITH: The reading was 2.9 micrograms. Of course, the cause of death is death due to acute poisoning narcosis by alcohol and meperidine, 2.9 micrograms.

DOCTOR GILMORE: Right.

CHIEF SMITH: Do you feel this is possible, that the drug you referred to—?

DOCTOR GILMORE: Meperidine is Lomotil.

CHIEF SMITH: —as Lomotil would show up to this degree?

DOCTOR GILMORE: I would just as soon you ask the—the—

CHIEF SMITH: Pathologist?

DOCTOR GILMORE: —pathologist because I'm—all I know is that it is—yes. It would be my impression, yes, especially since she bad been drinking and would have had a rapid absorption.

CHIEF SMITH: Would you have any idea what she would have injected herself with?

DOCTOR GILMORE: I told you. The only thing that she would have tried would have been Stadol. As I told you, she was afraid of Demerol. She was afraid of morphine. She was not afraid of Stadol, but I know—I know that she knew how to fill a syringe, but I have never known her to give herself a shot.

DETECTIVE HADLEY: If I may interrupt, Doctor, you made a statement a little while back that possibly your son may have tried to help out and just botched it up.

DOCTOR GILMORE: Oh, no. Oh, no.

DETECTIVE HADLEY: Is that incorrect?

DOCTOR GILMORE: That was incorrect. The only thing I mentioned was that my son and wife were home. I think she might well have decided not to make any noise and might possibly have tried to give herself a shot.

DETECTIVE HADLEY: You are saying she may have botched it up?

DOCTOR GILMORE: I think if anybody botched it up, Patty did. My son doesn't know—

DETECTIVE HADLEY: Your son is living in Florida now?

DOCTOR GILMORE: Yes.

DETECTIVE HADLEY: Do you know his address offhand?

DOCTOR GILMORE: No, but I can get it for you very easily.

CHIEF SMITH: You are aware, Doctor, we have the one syringe that—

DOCTOR GILMORE: Yes.

CHIEF SMITH: —the needle is missing.

DOCTOR GILMORE: Yes.

CHIEF SMITH: You referred to a bent needle in your—

DOCTOR GILMORE: In the ashtray.

CHIEF SMITH: That's in the ashtray—

DOCTOR GILMORE: That was in the ashtray in the hall.

CHIEF SMITH: —in the hall?

DOCTOR GILMORE: In the hallway.

CHIEF SMITH: Upstairs or—

DOCTOR GILMORE: Yeah, upstairs.

CHIEF SMITH: Do you keep in your bag or in your home any liquefied vitamin E at all?

DOCTOR GILMORE: Vitamin E?

CHIEF SMITH: Yeah.

DOCTOR GILMORE: No, but I think Patty was taking vitamin E.

CHIEF SMITH: In the normal form?

DOCTOR GILMORE: In tablet form.

CHIEF SMITH: In tablet form or—

DOCTOR GILMORE: I'm not sure. I know she was taking Centron or Surbex-T, which are vitamins. I don't know that—I have no idea whether she was taking vitamins, per se. Would you mind doing me a favor, sir. Could I use your phone?

MR. SUSS: Absolutely. Just dial 9 first. Then proceed.

(Stenographer's Note: At this point in the proceedings, Doctor Gilmore placed a telephone call.)

CHIEF SMITH: Can you give me an approximate time, Doctor, of when you discovered your wife—

DOCTOR GILMORE: Was dead?

CHIEF SMITH: Yes.

DOCTOR GILMORE: My guess, between 8:00 and 8:30.

CHIEF SMITH: Did you call anyone immediately or do you—

DOCTOR GILMORE: I called—I had my son call the ambulance. I think—I don't know when he called the police. I called her father.

CHIEF SMITH: After her body was taken to the Reading Hospital, did you have any contact with Doctor Glosser?

DOCTOR GILMORE: After it was taken to the hospital?

CHIEF SMITH: Yes.

DOCTOR GILMORE: No. When? Do you mean immediately after?

CHIEF SMITH: Yes.

DOCTOR GILMORE: No.

CHIEF SMITH: You didn't?

DOCTOR GILMORE: No.

CHIEF SMITH: You didn't call Doctor Glosser?

DOCTOR GILMORE: No.

CHIEF SMITH: Doctor Glosser didn't become involved until later that day; is that correct?

DOCTOR GILMORE: Correct, as far as I know. I did not call Doctor Glosser.

CHIEF SMITH: Had anyone notified the funeral director to come to the hospital, or was that —

DOCTOR GILMORE: I told the funeral director that there would be a post that he should contact—that he should make arrangements when the body was released.

CHIEF SMITH: Okay.

DETECTIVE HADLEY: Did Doctor Glosser call or contact you?

DOCTOR GILMORE: Doctor Glosser came out to see me.

DETECTIVE HADLEY: On the twenty-seventh, that day?

DOCTOR GILMORE: That evening. He called. He tried to get me at home and he said he was concerned about me because—I don't think he had my phone number. He came out and we discussed it. I told him I just felt that—the only thing I told him, I told him the same thing I told you gentlemen in regard to injectables in my bag. That's essentially what I told him.

CHIEF SMITH: Okay. Doctor Glosser was going to or did order an autopsy. This is correct, to your knowledge?

DOCTOR GILMORE: Oh, yes, as far as I know. Certainly.

CHIEF SMITH: Were you aware that he was leaving town the next day?

DOCTOR GILMORE: No.

CHIEF SMITH: Did you have any contact with Doctor John Meyers then?

DOCTOR GILMORE: Not John, Doctor John Meyers. I talked to the other gentleman, Doctor—you are talking about a coroner?

CHIEF SMITH: Yeah, the coroner.

DOCTOR GILMORE: No, no. I talked to one of the pathologists.

CHIEF SMITH: Okay. Did Doctor Glosser ever mention the police being present at an autopsy or not being present?

DOCTOR GILMORE: No.

CHIEF SMITH: And you don't know if he saw any reason to have the police present or not present at the time, Doctor?

DOCTOR GILMORE: No, I do not.

CHIEF SMITH: Okay. You had conversation with Doctor Keith at the pathology lab.

DOCTOR GILMORE: Yes.

CHIEF SMITH: That is correct?

DOCTOR GILMORE: Uh-huh.

CHIEF SMITH: That was the following day?

DOCTOR GILMORE: Yes, it was the following—I think I had two conversations. I think I had one the day of the post and the day after.

CHIEF SMITH: Did Doctor Keith advise you of any of his findings after the autopsy?

DOCTOR GILMORE: He told me he had found nothing on general autopsy that he ascribed death to, that he wanted to examine some bruises. Principally, I thought he just said the fact. Now I'm hearing more.

CHIEF SMITH: You understand, Doctor, the bruises which we feel were not explained and, of course—

DOCTOR GILMORE: Uh-huh. I understand that.

CHIEF SMITH: —it's apparent that some of the hemorrhages were quite large,—

DOCTOR GILMORE: Uh-huh.

CHIEF SMITH: —although they certainly did not cause death, according to the doctor.

DOCTOR GILMORE: I understand that.

CHIEF SMITH: If your wife had been outside and fallen, as you say, on the rear steps— they are concrete steps.

DOCTOR GILMORE: Yes.

CHIEF SMITH: It would have been an abrasion type.

DOCTOR GILMORE: Could well have been. If she fell on the steps on the inside, it would not have been, I don't think, because they are heavily rugged. The whole house is rugged.

CHIEF SMITH: Your son at no time mentioned hearing her fall—

DOCTOR GILMORE: No.

CHIEF SMITH: —not your daughter-in-law?

DOCTOR GILMORE: No, but I think they were probably quite well asleep, too. I don't know. I did not ask them. I don't know.

CHIEF SMITH: They apparently left her approximately 2:30 a.m., your daughter-in-law.

DOCTOR GILMORE: My daughter-in-law. My son, as I understand it, was already in bed. My daughter-in-law came up at 2:30, leaving her in the kitchen.

CHIEF SMITH: According to your daughter-in-law, your wife was left in the kitchen alone at 2:30 a.m.?

DOCTOR GILMORE: To the nearest of my recollection. It could well have—no. I think—I think at 2:00 a.m. she was left alone in the kitchen. I'm very sure of that, as sure as I can remember.

CHIEF SMITH: You mentioned someone heard her in your car. At what hour would that be?

DOCTOR GILMORE: The neighbors. When Patty would go out to the car, the dog would bark and she would talk to the dog, and my neighbors heard her go out to the car and come back. That's all they heard.

CHIEF SMITH: Was this after 2 a.m.?

DOCTOR GILMORE: It was—yes, it was after Linda—after the daughter-in-law had come upstairs.

CHIEF SMITH: You don't normally keep your medical bag in the house?

DOCTOR GILMORE: No. I keep it in the car.

CHIEF SMITH: And the car, or course, is locked.

DOCTOR GILMORE: No. The car is not locked, but my garage is locked.

CHIEF SMITH: But then she had to go into the garage.

DOCTOR GILMORE: Oh, yes. The door is locked. The garage door will only go up with a button, but the door that opens into the garage from the patio is unlocked.

CHIEF SMITH: Okay. Your wife was evidently undressed prior to going to bed.

DOCTOR GILMORE: She was dressed in bed the way she – she had night clothing on.

CHIEF SMITH: And she hung her clothing up that she had worn the night before?

DOCTOR GILMORE: It wasn't hung up. It was draped over a chair—

CHIEF SMITH: Draped over a chair?

DOCTOR GILMORE: —but that was not new.

CHIEF SMITH: You understand our concern, Doctor?

DOCTOR GILMORE: Certainly I understand your concern.

CHIEF SMITH: I mean, the injuries are—

DOCTOR GILMORE: I understand your concern. The injuries could only have been produced by a fall, someone striking her, someone being me. I am possibly—

CHIEF SMITH: No. As I say, we are not pointing—

DOCTOR GILMORE: No. I know that, but that house was full of happiness, my friend, until the morning, and I don't want to hear anything about this being a suicide because my wife—

CHIEF SMITH: Doctor, we haven't mentioned anything. You understand, I'm—

DOCTOR GILMORE: Okay.

CHIEF SMITH: —I'm only going by what the autopsy report says.

DOCTOR GILMORE: Good enough.

CHIEF SMITH: I'm sure she wouldn't have inflicted anything like this.

DOCTOR GILMORE: No.

CHIEF SMITH: That isn't what—

DOCTOR GILMORE: Frankly, I think she would have fallen in her bedroom or in her dressing room because my wife would be a little—let's face it. She had 2-point-something alcohol and she has been known to fall more than once and she could have fallen in her bedroom or in her dressing room, which is a soft rug, and I don't think really anybody would have heard. If—I certainly didn't, and that—and that room is quite well built and I'm not—I don't think anyone would have—I'm not sure. It would be in my mind that no one would have heard her.

CHIEF SMITH: Of course, if she had—is there furniture there she could have struck herself on?

DOCTOR GILMORE: Yes. There is also bathroom furniture. There is a chair. There is a table. We are talking about her dressing room. She could have fallen downstairs. When you come out of the kitchen, you come onto a hard surface with one step up that is damn hard. She could have fallen there because it was not uncommon for her to fall and she would wake up in the morning and say "Where did I get this bruise?" or "Where did I get this bruise?" That was not uncommon.

DETECTIVE HADLEY: The Amorosos you were having supper at, is that River Road?

DOCTOR GILMORE: No. It's Mat Amoroso. He has the Amoroso—

CHIEF SMITH: Decorating.

DOCTOR GILMORE: Decorating.

CHIEF SMITH: Who all was there at that supper?

DOCTOR GILMORE: Mr. And Mrs. Amoroso, my son and daughter-in-law, Patty and myself.

DETECTIVE HADLEY: Anybody else?

DOCTOR GILMORE: Nobody else.

SERGEANT FRANTZ: There is no question, prior to you going to bed that night, Doc, she definitely did not have any bruises on her at that time?

DOCTOR GILMORE: None at all. No. No.

SERGEANT FRANTZ: So they would have had to occur after you went to bed?

DOCTOR GILMORE: Yes. It would have to.

SERGEANT FRANTZ: After you went to bed?

DOCTOR GILMORE: After I went to bed.

DETECTIVE HADLEY: Would it be common for her to wear makeup to bed?

DOCTOR GILMORE: Yes.

DETECTIVE HADLEY: Would she wear mascara when she went to bed at night?

DOCTOR GILMORE: Oh, yes, indeed. She wanted to look good.

SERGEANT FRANTZ: And the doctor's case was definitely in the car when you went to bed?

DOCTOR GILMORE: Oh, yes.

SERGEANT FRANTZ: And she had to go out and bring it in—

DOCTOR GILMORE: The bag was in the car.

SERGEANT FRANTZ: That particular night.

CHIEF SMITH: No one else mentioned the injuries to your son

or daughter-in-law?

DOCTOR GILMORE: No. No one at all.

CHIEF SMITH: And, of course, as you say, they discovered it. They didn't awaken during the night that you know of or they didn't hear you?

DOCTOR GILMORE: No. They were just as surprised as I was when I informed them.

MR. SUSS: Doctor, have you had an opportunity to read the autopsy report?

DOCTOR GILMORE: No, I haven't.

MR. SUSS: Would you like to do so at this time?

DOCTOR GILMORE: Yes.

(Stenographer's Note: At this point in the proceedings, a document was handed to Doctor Gilmore.)

DOCTOR GILMORE: When I say here that she might have used Stadol and Compazine, it probably shouldn't say, and found that. It would have been my impression that the only two drugs she would have taken would have been Stadol which is for pain and Compazine which is for nausea, but to my mind there was not enough missing of either drug that I felt that any had been taken.

MR. SUSS: Was your bag the only possible source she had for those medications?

DOCTOR GILMORE: Only injectable drugs with the—any injectable drug, absolutely. I always keep them in my bag. I don't even have a place in the office where I lock them. Is it really necessary that I read this? [*indicating*]

MR. SUSS: If you would prefer not to, it's not necessary.

DOCTOR GILMORE: Okay.

MR. SUSS: Now, Doctor, Demerol, is that a brand name or a generic name?

DOCTOR GILMORE: Demerol is a brand name.

MR. SUSS: What is the generic name?

DOCTOR GILMORE: Meperedine. Demerol is made by Winthrop.

MR. SUSS: What is the generic description of Lomotil?

DOCTOR GILMORE: That is a brand name.

MR. SUSS: What is the generic equivalent?

DOCTOR GILMORE: I have always ordered Lomotil, the brand name. Diphenoxylate hydrochloride, 2.5 milligrams.

MR. SUSS: What were the possible sources of either Demerol or the generic equivalent of meperedine within the household?

DOCTOR GILMORE: The only source would have been injectable Demerol in my bag. There were no tablets. That would be the only source of Demerol.

MR. SUSS: Did you have sufficient quantities in your bag to have produced a reading of 2.9 micrograms per deciliter?

DOCTOR GILMORE: Did I have sufficient quantities in my bag?

MR. SUSS: That it would have, and she gained access to it, produced a toxicology report which reflects the meperedine concentration of 2.9 micrograms.

DOCTOR GILMORE: Would you mind letting me state that another way?

MR. SUSS: Any way you prefer, sir.

DOCTOR GILMORE: I had enough in my possession to do that, but there was not that amount missing.

DETECTIVE HADLEY: How many cc's—

DOCTOR GILMORE: One cc.

DETECTIVE HADLEY: How many cc's would be a normal dosage?

DOCTOR GILMORE: One cc. That's an injectable. There was only one cc missing, and I am almost positive I can name the patient I gave it to the day before for a migraine. Other than that, it was a full bottle. For your information, there was another full bottle in my desk which had been unopened at home.

CHIEF SMITH: How many pills of this Lomotil would it take to perhaps—you would know the equivalent.

DOCTOR GILMORE: I know that she had been apparently been taking Lomotil probably for nine days from what she told me, and my—it's a meperedine-like drug, and I think that—again, check the pathologist. I don't think it can be differentiated in a laboratory study. She made one statement when I told her to try Imodium, "It has always worked and it will work," and, knowing her temper, if she developed diarrhea, she could have easily taken—I don't know how many because—I don't know. I just don't know, but she had a temper.

DETECTIVE HADLEY: Would she have taken these perhaps before she went—

DOCTOR GILMORE: Into bed?

DETECTIVE HADLEY: —to bed?

DOCTOR GILMORE: Yeah.

DETECTIVE HADLEY: It's quite apparent she evidently injected herself prior to going to bed.

DOCTOR GILMORE: Well, she at least tried, but I would like to know what the skin samples show of any drug, and I would also like to know why it didn't show up in the toxicology. Unless it was Demerol, and it wasn't Demerol. I would give you a hundred to one—that's stupid. I don't think they are going to be able to show you any Demerol in her skin. I'd bet my life on it.

MR. SUSS: Doctor, did I understand you to say that Lomotil will produce results such that this toxicology examination could have reflected it as meperedine?

DOCTOR GILMORE: You are correct.

MR. SUSS: Does the Lomotil have an effect comparable to

meperedine or is it only in analysis confusing with meperedine? Do you understand the difference?

DOCTOR GILMORE: You don't—you don't—we give paregoric for diarrhea. That's camphorated tincture of opium. Now then, we give Demerol injectable usually for migraine headache, frequently for coronary occlusion. What I'm saying is that Lomotil is cumulative. It will last for thirty hours. I think that, if she took a given number—I'm not sure how much—that it would have the same effect as an overdose of Demerol given intramuscularly because she had been drinking and alcohol will take any drug directly into the circulating blood.

MR. SUSS: Did I understand you to say that she had indicated to you that she had been taking the Lomotil for diarrhea over a period of some nine days?

DOCTOR GILMORE: She said she had diarrhea for nine days. I asked her, "What are you doing?" She said, "Lomotil." I said, "Why don't you try Imodium," and she said, "Because it doesn't work," and that was Wednesday, and I said,—she said, "Don't worry. It always has worked before. It will work," or words to that effect. In other words, go to hell with your Imodium.

MR. SUSS: Now, do I recall that she had had a past either personal or medicinal hostility to Demerol? Did I understand you to say that at some point?

DOCTOR GILMORE: Yes. Yes, because it made her very ill, plus she was very afraid of narcotics.

MR. SUSS: When you were suggesting the alternative to Lomotil on Wednesday night,—

DOCTOR GILMORE: Uh-huh.

MR. SUSS: —the alternative which she ultimately rejected and said, go to hell with the alternative,—

DOCTOR GILMORE: Uh-huh.

MR. SUSS: —did you mention to her at that time the similarities in effect between the Lomotil she was choosing to take and the Demerol to which she was always in the past hostile?

DOCTOR GILMORE: I think she would have known that because I was sued for giving a baby—it was a mistake—Lomotil, and I—during that time—I thought it was a two-year-old baby. It turned out to be a two month old, and I thoroughly went over it with her with the drug and told her the problem that that Lomotil had the same effects as giving, in essence, small amounts of Demerol and atropine.

MR. SUSS: When was this incident with the baby?

DOCTOR GILMORE: This was several years ago. It was a malpractice suit which has since been settled. I don't—I don't know that I reinforced it at that moment. I don't think I did. To tell you the truth, I didn't even think about it because she—you know—she felt—you know, she felt quite sure that this was going to work. She didn't worry about it. Besides, she was in a hurry. She had to go and get my son and daughter-in-law.

CHIEF SMITH: Doctor, regressing, where did she pick up your son and daughter-in-law?

DOCTOR GILMORE: Reading Airport.

CHIEF SMITH: At the Reading airport. That was on a Wednesday?

DOCTOR GILMORE: Wednesday afternoon.

CHIEF SMITH: Wednesday afternoon. Okay. She hadn't seen your son or daughter-in-law for several months?

DOCTOR GILMORE: Oh, no. It's been—yeah. I think we were down last Christmas to see them. I think they were up—I can't say that for sure. I think they have been up since that time, but they were up once this summer.

CHIEF SMITH: There was no problem, no domestic problems,

between any of you, your son—?

DOCTOR GILMORE: Oh, no. They were very fond of each other.

CHIEF SMITH: Your wife and your son? Very well. Of course, as you say, they accompanied you. They were with you the whole evening.

DOCTOR GILMORE: The whole evening.

CHIEF SMITH: You didn't drink with them when you came home, correct?

DOCTOR GILMORE: Oh, no. I went straight home. I went straight to bed.

CHIEF SMITH: They stayed downstairs and evidently had a drink or two.

DOCTOR GILMORE: Yeah. I think they had—might have had a drink or two, but my son drinks only beer. My daughter-in-law is pregnant in her second month. I think she might have had a little wine. I think Patty was having some beer. At least, that's what was on the table.

CHIEF SMITH: Okay. Another reason, 0.24, as you know, is quite high, you know, of blood alcohol. It's really quite high.

DOCTOR GILMORE: Uh-huh. Well, she had—I think she drank DeWars and water before we ate. I don't know how many. She had a fair amount of wine. It was a red wine, and I think she had beer when we got home. There was a glass unfinished. I don't know how many beers she had.

CHIEF SMITH: So, if she would take Lomotil and perhaps take it with beer, would that produce—would the effects be much greater or would that make any difference?

DOCTOR GILMORE: I don't think she took it with beer. I think she had enough. You must remember that, if you have nothing, very little, in your stomach and you take anything with an alcohol or close to it, the absorption is different. That's why we have elixir drugs. If you take an elixir of phenobarbital—alcohol is the only substance immediately absorbed so it's the closest to giving an injectable that you can come to. It's absorbed immediately through the stomach.

CHIEF SMITH: So our feeling is right now she evidently took Lomotil for perhaps her diarrhea condition and—

DOCTOR GILMORE: I think she was angry and probably took too many.

CHIEF SMITH: —took too many. The needle marks you really can't say other than perhaps something for her headache that she may have.

DOCTOR GILMORE: I think—I think that the pathologist should be able to tell that in the skin. If he can find nothing, it would sort of substantiate what I think. I think she was unsuccessful in giving the Stadol.

CHIEF SMITH: It would be Stadol?

DOCTOR GILMORE: It would be Stadol.

CHIEF SMITH: Would that have been in a vial type, something in a vial, or would she have disposed of something?

DOCTOR GILMORE: You know I have the bottle.

CHIEF SMITH: It's a liquid that she could put in a syringe?

DOCTOR GILMORE: Correct.

CHIEF SMITH: She could have removed this liquid from your bag and you probably are not—you wouldn't be aware of the small amount she would have taken?

DOCTOR GILMORE: If it were any—remember, the dose for Stadol is two cc's. The bottle only holds ten, so I definitely would have noticed a decrease.

CHIEF SMITH: You would have noticed that?

DOCTOR GILMORE: I would have noticed the decrease. The significance in the toxicology would be telling us something about

Stadol because I told him the name of the drug.

CHIEF SMITH: That is a nonnarcotic drug?

DOCTOR GILMORE: That is a nonnarcotic drug.

CHIEF SMITH: So that wouldn't really reflect in their toxology report.

DOCTOR GILMORE: I wouldn't know why not. It's a drug.

CHIEF SMITH: But they were giving a drug screen for narcotic drugs.

DOCTOR GILMORE: Alcohol is not a narcotic drug either but it's on there. Okay, but I gave them that drug.

CHIEF SMITH: Then you did notice or you didn't notice a difference in your vial, or did you check?

DOCTOR GILMORE: I noticed no difference in the Demerol, no difference in morphine. I would not swear to Stadol—

CHIEF SMITH: Okay. That's what I mean.

DOCTOR GILMORE: —but I would swear to this: No more that one cc.

CHIEF SMITH: No more than one cc?

DOCTOR GILMORE: Yes.

CHIEF SMITH: —is that what you are saying?

DOCTOR GILMORE: I am saying my—my—my bet is she didn't even get the one cc, knowing her temper.

CHIEF SMITH: But that is very unusual for her to administer?

DOCTOR GILMORE: Totally unusual. Never, never, never, never would suspect. I think she asked Marsha, her girlfriend, one time to give her a shot and loaded the needle with Stadol because I was asleep, and Marsha refused to give it, so she did know how to load the needle. She did know how to load the syringe.

DETECTIVE HADLEY: The syringe that was obtained, Doctor, was—

DOCTOR GILMORE: Two cc.

DETECTIVE HADLEY: Multi-fit?

DOCTOR GILMORE: Two cc syringe. You know, you would have to fill that up a number of times.

DETECTIVE HADLEY: Is that normal for you—

DOCTOR GILMORE: I use a two cc syringe for aqueous solutions, Demerol, Stadol, Compazine, because they are all aqueous and the smaller they are the less it hurts. I have a five cc syringe with a much larger gauge needle for the use of penicillin, and of the thicker injectables that are given, so they don't get stuck in a small area.

CHIEF SMITH: You didn't notice anything in the bathroom or dressing room knocked over, anything she could have fallen against?

DOCTOR GILMORE: I didn't notice. I wasn't looking. I really knew nothing about bruises. I would—I would say that her room was not disheveled, but there is a large bathtub that's built in. I suppose she could have hit, but I noticed nothing. If that's what you are asking, but then again, I wasn't looking.

CHIEF SMITH: We are looking for something blunt, you understand.

DOCTOR GILMORE: That could be a stair. It could easily be a stair. Was it braised or was it a bruise?

CHIEF SMITH: It's a bruise.

DOCTOR GILMORE: If it's a bruise, it could be the steps going upstairs because it's heavily rugged and she could have fallen forward very easily. I think you referred to something on the back of her head.

CHIEF SMITH: Yes.

DOCTOR GILMORE: That could have been a fall on the—on the—on her dressing room floor.

CHIEF SMITH: There is also one on the front of her forehead.

DOCTOR GILMORE: That could be coming up steps, too, and there is a full—if you have ever been in the dressing room, there is a full-length mirror that takes two-thirds of the wall, so I'm sure if she did try to inject herself with the lights on, she would certainly have a full view.

CHIEF SMITH: In a distance how many feet would your son's room or the guest room have been from her dressing room?

DOCTOR GILMORE: Well, it's right next door,—

CHIEF SMITH: Right next door?

DOCTOR GILMORE: —but there's a closet that separates the wall full of clothing with a slide door that is glass. It is glass.

CHIEF SMITH: You don't know if their door was open or closed?

DOCTOR GILMORE: I would assume when she came up the stairs—my door was closed, I would assume, because I closed it when I went to bed. I would assume that theirs was closed because they are man and wife and I—you know.

CHIEF SMITH: It's possible she could have fallen or there could have been noise without them—

DOCTOR GILMORE: Absolutely, on those rugs.

CHIEF SMITH: —without them being aware of it?

DOCTOR GILMORE: Uh-huh.

DETECTIVE HADLEY: —Was she right-handed or left-handed?

DOCTOR GILMORE: Me?

DETECTIVE HADLEY: Patty.

DOCTOR GILMORE: Patty? Right-handed.

DETECTIVE HADLEY: You are right-handed?

DOCTOR GILMORE: I write right-handed. Not very well with that, but—

CHIEF SMITH: Doctor, as you know we had the syringe.

DOCTOR GILMORE: Yes.

CHIEF SMITH: We had that analyzed at the State Police Lab.

DOCTOR GILMORE: Uh-huh.

CHIEF SMITH: They came up with a finding that there was what they suspect to be vitamin E in this syringe.

DOCTOR GILMORE: That syringe could have had—I don't carry any vitamin E. I use—there is a possibility it could have been some B complex in the vial.

CHIEF SMITH: Some vitamin,—

DOCTOR GILMORE: Okay.

CHIEF SMITH: He thought perhaps maybe more like E.

DOCTOR GILMORE: I don't carry vitamin E. I do carry B complex. It could have been that.

CHIEF SMITH: There would have been no reason for her to take or could she have taken this by mistake? Do you have a vial of vitamins or something that she could have used it by mistake?

DOCTOR GILMORE: I have sometimes given her vitamin B complex because it does help with nausea.

CHIEF SMITH: That will.

DOCTOR GILMORE: B complex. Beautiful for nausea.

CHIEF SMITH: She could have—

DOCTOR GILMORE: She could have given herself B complex. Never thought of it.

CHIEF SMITH: Okay. You understand, Doctor, there were many questions we need to ask you

DOCTOR GILMORE: Listen, Listen, this is just as important to me.

CHIEF SMITH: It's important to you. It's important to, you know, everyone—

DOCTOR GILMORE: I know.

CHIEF SMITH: —and it's important to the district attorney's office, and we would certainly like to clear this—

DOCTOR GILMORE: Uh-huh.

CHIEF SMITH: —and, as I say,—

DOCTOR GILMORE: Any—

CHIEF SMITH: —the coroner's office didn't help us clear it up. It became muddled through their report.

DOCTOR GILMORE: Anything more I think of I will gladly inform you or anything more you want to know from me—if you want, what do you call it, a lie detector test,—

CHIEF SMITH: No. We are not asking,—

DOCTOR GILMORE: —I will gladly take it.

CHIEF SMITH: —but, as you know, Doctor Meyers made a statement to the press that she aspirated her nose which we find certainly nothing in here whatsoever.

DOCTOR GILMORE: I think that happens in every death. The thing that makes me think about Lomotil, quite frankly, gentlemen, is—I'm a deputy coroner. I don't think I have ever attended a death where the bed hasn't been wet. Lomotil would have prevented that.

CHIEF SMITH: Lomotil would have prevented the bed from having—

DOCTOR GILMORE: Because it has an atropine effect, and it could have prevented emptying the bladder.

CHIEF SMITH: And there was no fluid on the bed?

DOCTOR GILMORE: None at all. No bowel movement, no fluid. Just moisture where her head was. And it was ringed, I'm sure, with the color of wine.

CHIEF SMITH: Okay. You didn't receive any calls during the night, no emergency calls?

DOCTOR GILMORE: No.

CHIEF SMITH: Nothing like that?

DOCTOR GILMORE: What night?

CHIEF SMITH: That same night.

DOCTOR GILMORE: No, no. If you would like to check that out,—

CHIEF SMITH: No, I'm just asking.

DOCTOR GILMORE: The medical building we have, but I didn't receive any.

CHIEF SMITH: Barry, do you have anything you would like?

DETECTIVE HADLEY: If we could have possibly your son's address in Florida and phone number—

DOCTOR GILMORE: Would you mind picking it up at the office tomorrow?

CHIEF SMITH: That's okay.

DETECTIVE HADLEY: That would be all right.

MR. SUSS: Could we have that packet of Lomotil?

DOCTOR GILMORE: Yeah. Don't take it.

CHIEF SMITH: I don't think—

DOCTOR GILMORE: Do yourself a favor, lock it up in the PDR; okay?

SERGEANT FRANTZ: What time did you go to bed?

DOCTOR GILMORE: My guess is 12:30 to 1:00.

SERGEANT FRANTZ: And when you woke up, it was about what time?

DOCTOR GILMORE: I would say somewhere around 9:00.

SERGEANT FRANTZ: Is that the first time you woke up,—

DOCTOR GILMORE: Yeah. I don't think earlier—

SERGEANT FRANTZ: And you heard nothing in between there?

DOCTOR GILMORE: No way.

CHIEF SMITH: Is there anything you would like to ask us, Doctor?

DOCTOR GILMORE: No. I'm just sick about the whole damn thing.

DETECTIVE HADLEY: I understand.

DOCTOR GILMORE: You know, I feel so relieved because they found a drug and I think I can explain it and I couldn't before. That's all I can say. Is it okay if I go? Number one, I've got to go to the john. Number two—I don't know how many damn house calls I have.

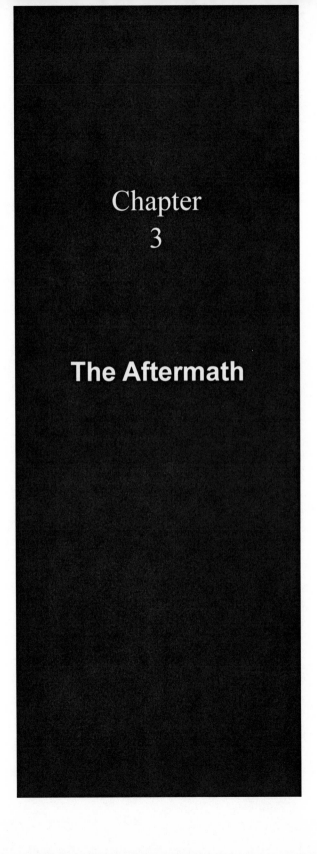

Chapter
3

The Aftermath

Among the regulars at the Whit-Mar Inn was Barrie Pease, a member of the Pennsylvania State Police, assigned as a criminal investigator to the white-collar crime unit since March 1980. Pease was, at the time, a member of the state police for 14 years, but was not involved at all in any investigation of the Patty Gilmore death, but would become an important witness during the coming legal morass because of his friendship with the Gilmores.

He knew Doctor Gilmore since about 1974, first meeting the doctor in his (Doctor Gilmore's) capacity as a deputy coroner and in Pease's capacity as a criminal investigator with the state police.

Inn owner Harry Kore is the person who told Pease about Patty's death. He didn't see Gilmore until about a week after her death when they had a brief conversation at the inn. Pease used the opportunity to say how sorry he was to hear about Patty. He noticed that Gilmore was emotionally upset.

Later during the hearings and trial, Pease would be subjected to intense questioning about his meetings and conversations with Gilmore during this period.

Around the fifteenth of December, about a week to ten days after that brief conversation, Pease again saw Gilmore at the inn. That conversation was lengthy. While they were sitting at the end of the bar, Pease recalled that Gilmore told him that he had been at the district attorney's office where they had been questioning him about Patty's death, and that somebody in that office thought he had killed Patty. Gilmore said Stuart Suss, assistant district attorney, Muhlenberg Police Chief Harley Smith and Muhlenberg Detective Barry Hadley conducted the interview session on December 11.

According to Pease, Gilmore was still emotionally upset

during that conversation, and although he wasn't intoxicated, he suspected that the alcohol was starting to affect him.

Pease also said that Gilmore told him that Patty had died from an overdose of Demerol and a high blood-alcohol content; that the night before she died, she had been sick and had been vomiting and had diarrhea. He told Pease that he gave her an injection the evening or early morning of the twenty-sixth or twenty-seventh to take care of the vomiting and the sickness from the alcohol. Pease later said he didn't recall Gilmore telling him what Patty's specific alcohol content was, only that it was a high level. He wasn't sure whether that was Gilmore's term or whether it was his. Pease testified that Gilmore did not describe Patty's condition as just having a lot to drink, nor did he state where Patty had been drinking.

He understood Gilmore to say that he gave her a dose of vitamin B-12, and also a drug that Pease never heard of—meperidine. Pease was unaware that the brand name for meperidine is Demerol. He said Gilmore also mentioned a drug named Lomotil, a drug used to treat diarrhea. Pease confirmed during his testimony that Gilmore stated that he gave Patty an injection of vitamin B-12 and meperidine the evening or early morning of her death, November 26 or 27. He said, when questioned, that he never remembered hearing the name of the substance meperidine before Gilmore mentioned it to him, and that the Muhlenberg Police never mentioned the drug's name to him.

Gilmore told Pease that he didn't think he had killed Patty and that he couldn't live with himself if he had killed her. Gilmore talked about how he would give Patty injections if she had been out and drank too much. Pease got the impression that Patty regularly got sick if she had too much to drink, and then Gilmore would routinely give her the injection to straighten her out. While they were having this conversation, Kore, who was bartending, would come over between customers and stand next to Gilmore. He was there for part of the conversation and gone for part of it. Pease assumed that Kore was able to hear at least parts of the conversation, although Pease didn't know which parts he overheard. Pease said that he didn't recall Kore saying anything during the conversation.

Then Gilmore mentioned to Pease that he had a pistol at home and he wasn't sure how to use it and how to take the safety off. Pease told Gilmore that he didn't think it was a good idea considering his state of mind, in a very distraught condition, that he have a firearm in his house. He suggested that Gilmore give it to him until he decides whom he wants to give it to.

Pease and Gilmore then left the Whit-Mar Inn in Doctor Gilmore's car and drove to his house. Pease recalled that Gilmore was still emotionally upset, but not too intoxicated to drive. Pease stated that he would not have let Gilmore drive if he had had too much to drink. Pease did state that he thought Gilmore's abuse of alcohol was becoming a problem since Patty's death. Gilmore went into the house, went upstairs, and removed the .32 caliber revolver from the headboard of the bed. He also gave Pease a box of bullets. Pease unloaded the weapon, and left the house with the pistol and box of bullets.

Pease didn't see Gilmore again until December 22, the day before he left the state for the holidays. The conversation on the twenty-second was held at Gilmore's house after he told Pease that he would like to give the pistol to his son Barry, who was visiting from Florida for the holidays. Pease took the pistol to Gilmore's house and explained to Barry how to take the gun to a gun dealer and transfer the registration into his name.

Patty had told Pease about two weeks before her death that Barry and Linda Gilmore would be visiting from Florida, and that Patty would be cooking Thanksgiving dinner for a group of people. Pease learned that Barry and Linda were present at the Gilmore house on November 27 when Barry came into the Whit-Mar Inn a few days later to cancel the Gilmore's scheduled Christmas party.

Immediately after Pease gave Barry the pistol downstairs around 6:30 p.m. on the twenty-second, Gilmore asked Pease if he could talk to him upstairs. He took him up to the hallway at the top of the stairs and showed him the bedroom that he had shared with Patty, which was on the left side of the hallway as you enter. Despite the obvious fact that Gilmore had been drinking and had a martini in his hand, and was weeping and showing the signs of being emotionally upset that he had displayed during their previous meetings, Pease didn't think he was intoxicated during this meeting at the house.

He told Pease that on that fateful night, or the morning when he woke up and the police had come, Patty had been lying diagonally across the bed next to him. Lying next to her was a stethoscope; on the headboard of the bed was a cotton ball with some bloodstains on it, and there was a syringe with a bent needle in a grayish-colored ashtray on the nightstand next to the bed.

He told Pease that he threw the syringe away, threw the cotton ball away, and moved the ashtray from the nightstand to a small table that was in the hall outside the bedroom, and that he put the stethoscope back into his medical bag, and then wasn't sure if he moved the medical bag from the study into Patty's dressing room or from the dressing room into the study.

After Pease returned to Pennsylvania after the holidays,

sometime during the first two weeks of January, he contacted Chief Smith and briefed him on what he knew about Patty Gilmore's death.

Pease later testified that Gilmore told him that he had not told the district attorney's office about the stethoscope or the cotton ball or about moving the ashtray. Pease asked Gilmore if he told the district attorney's office about injecting Patty with meperidine. Pease testified that he didn't remember getting any response to that question. At this time Gilmore told Pease that he had been referred to Reading lawyer Emmanuel Dimitriou, known as one of the best defense attorneys in the country. Pease advised Gilmore to go see Dimitriou and tell him the whole story

Dimitriou was definitely the man Doctor Gilmore needed to see immediately because on Friday morning, June 19, 1981 homicide charges were filed against him in the death of his wife on Thanksgiving morning the previous year.

Chapter
4

The Murder Charge

The formal complaint filed on June 19, 1981, stated that Doctor Gilmore, whose age was listed as fifty-nine, killed his wife by injecting her five times in the buttocks with the drug meperidine, a depressant, while she was intoxicated. He was arraigned before District Judge George Wenger in Reading District Court. The arraignment was held before Wenger because Temple's District Judge Doris Dorminy was reportedly ill. Wenger set a tentative preliminary hearing date for the following Friday before Dorminy.

Muhlenberg Police Chief Smith stated that it took until June to file the charges because the investigation took a considerable amount of time retaining "the best forensic people we could get," and the need to appoint a special prosecutor.

The case had originally been ruled an accidental death by Doctor William Glosser, the Berks County acting coroner. Glosser would soon come under investigation as a result of his controversial ruling.

Detective Hadley charged Gilmore with criminal homicide, aggravated assault, and recklessly endangering another person. Gilmore surrendered at 9 a.m. with attorney Dimitriou and posted $50,000 bail.

Berks County attorney Charles Haddad, appointed as special deputy by state attorney general LeRoy Zimmerman, made the surprising announcement that Glosser's role in the case was being investigated. According to a statement released at the arraignment, Haddad was appointed after District Attorney George Yatron, son of longtime congressman Gus Yatron, requested to be relieved from the case due to his and his staff's close contact and association with Doctor Gilmore while Gilmore served as a deputy coroner.

The court documents filed stated that about 8:30 a.m. on

November 27, 1980, Gilmore reported the death of his wife. Doctor George Kershner pronounced her dead at 9:40 a.m. at the Reading Hospital.

Doctor John Keith, a pathologist at the hospital who performed the autopsy, reported that Patty Gilmore had suffered a black eye, bruises about the face, and two scalp hemorrhages, one in the front and one in the back of her head. Keith also confirmed that Patty had a blood alcohol level of 0.24, and a high concentration of meperidine. He confirmed that there were five fresh needle marks on her right buttock. Keith had received his bachelor of science degree in pre-medical and liberal arts from the University of Geneva, Geneva, Switzerland. He also received his medical degree at the university, and was certified by the American Board of Pathology. He did four years of specialty training in anatomic pathology at Washington University School of Medicine, St. Louis, Missouri. He was licensed to practice medicine in Pennsylvania since 1973, and was employed by the Reading Hospital since May, 1973.

Doctor Keith listed the cause of death as "toxicology pending," which meant that further analysis was necessary.

Despite Keith's findings, Doctor Glosser issued a death certificate the next day certifying the cause of death as accidental due to choking on her own vomit, and the time of death at between 3:00 and 3:30 a.m. After issuing the death certificate Glosser reportedly ordered Keith not to send any blood samples to any laboratory for further study, and to destroy the existing blood samples.

Instead, Keith sent the blood samples to Doctor Fredrick Rieders and Doctor William Cohn, at the National Medical Services, Inc., Willow Grove, Pennsylvania, for analysis. He also sent them the body tissue that contained the five needle marks.

Rieders and Cohn reported that Patty's death was caused by acute meperidine poisoning caused by multiple injections of the drug in the buttocks. Their report also concluded that the amount of meperidine in Patty's body was enough to cause vital body functions to cease.

Court documents also recounted the December 11 interview with Gilmore conducted by Detective Hadley, Chief Smith, and assistant district attorney Suss. The defendant at that time denied giving his wife any injections of meperidine and also said he didn't believe his wife gave herself the injections. He also denied causing any bruises on his wife's body.

Other facts about the case were released when the charges were filed on June 19. It was revealed, after the state police entered the investigation, that on December 14 or 15 that Gilmore told Trooper Barrie Pease about giving Patty injections of vitamin B complex and meperidine, and that a week later on December 22 Gilmore told state police that on the morning of Patty's death he threw a syringe and a cotton ball with bloodstains away. It was at this time that the public was told that Gilmore never phoned police on Thanksgiving morning, but just phoned for an ambulance to take his wife to the hospital. Muhlenberg Patrolman Dougherty responded only because he heard the ambulance call on the police radio. The implication was that Doctor Gilmore, a deputy coroner, with the assistance of Doctor Glosser, county coroner, never intended to get the police involved at all in Patty's death.

Just a couple of days after the Gilmore charges were filed, authorities announced that they were launching an investigation of acting county coroner Doctor William Glosser. He was scheduled to be questioned the following week about why he issued the ruling of accidental death of Patty Gilmore, who was later found to have died of sedative poisoning. Glosser had stated that Patty died of suffocation, choking on her own vomit.

To add to Doctor Glosser's troubles, the Berks County Republican executive committee called for him to withdraw from the November elections as a candidate for a full term as coroner because of his controversial involvement in the Gilmore murder case. Doctor Glosser rejected the committee's request.

Chapter
5

The Defender

Doctor Gilmore had the financial resources to post $50,000 bail and to hire a competent lawyer to defend him. He had allowed himself to be interviewed at length by the authorities without the benefit of having a lawyer present, a very dangerous thing to do.

He couldn't have found a better attorney when he was referred to Reading defense specialist Emmanuel Dimitriou. Known by everyone as "Manny," Dimitriou was enjoying an illustrious and lucrative career defending clients in high-profile cases. He was the head of his own law firm that specialized in criminal defense, including DUI and traffic offenses, drug offenses, sex offenses, theft offenses, property offenses, and Internet offenses. Eventually his daughter and son-in-law, both attorneys, joined the firm, located on Court Street in Reading.

After being admitted to the bar in 1960, Manny really began his career as Pennsylvania's first public defender in 1964 when the state instituted its public defender act. He served as Berks County, Pennsylvania's first public defender, serving in that post from 1964 until May 1968. A committee that included future Berks County judge Albert Stallone selected him for the job. According to news reports at the time, Stallone said, "There was not doubt in my mind that he was by far the best possible candidate that we could have picked." Stallone further commented, "Manny was cut out to do criminal defense work. We knew he had tremendous ability."

If an accused person can't afford to hire a lawyer from the private legal community, the court can appoint a government-paid lawyer called a public defender to represent the accused. To qualify to have a public defender, the accused must convince the judge that he or she can't afford to hire an attorney on his own. The judge may ask for details about financial resources, assets, income, and debts. The accused may also need to provide the court with documentation such as pay stubs to prove income level.

Manny, the father of seven children, was born in Kos, Greece, in 1933, the son of Greek immigrants Haralampis and Ekaterina Dimitriou. Raised in the South Reading neighborhood surrounding Pearl Street, which even still today has a secluded old-world look that features clean narrow streets and block after block of small row houses, corner bars, and tiny grocery stores, a bistro thick with ethnic culture scattered here and there, and of course anchored by the Catholic Church and School—concrete shelters that provide stability while overlooking the families as they worship, baptize, marry, and bury their members.

Manny, a product of this neighborhood, graduated from Reading High School in Reading, Franklin and Marshall College, Lancaster, Pennsylvania, and Dickinson School of Law, Carlisle, Pennsylvania. He served two years in the United States Army. He was a devoted Philadelphia Eagles fan, and was a proud member of the Wednesday "spaghetti with the boys" night.

Doctor Gilmore was in good hands as Manny Dimitriou's client. He was recognized as a stellar criminal trial attorney in Pennsylvania, trying cases throughout the state. He was listed in *Best Lawyers in America* every year since its publication in 1983, was admitted to practice before the Pennsylvania Supreme Court, U.S. District Court for the Eastern District and the Middle District of Pennsylvania, and the U.S. Third Circuit Court of Appeals and the U.S. Supreme Court. Manny served as a vice-chairman of the Pennsylvania Supreme Court Criminal Rules Committee.

When interviewed for this book, retired president judge Forrest Schaeffer, who presided at the Gilmore trial, spoke warmly of Manny Dimitriou. Schaeffer said his willingness to sit down and discuss the issues of a case—and always prepared to compromise while at the same time representing his client's best interests—contributed to his irreproachable reputation.

He was an active member of SS Constantine and Helen Greek Orthodox Church in Reading, and was a lecturer at Penn State University, Alvernia College, and Albright College.

There are many people who associate defense attorneys with the clients they represent. For some it's easy to look with contempt at a lawyer who would defend despicable persons such as murderers, thieves, and drug dealers. This is a classic showing of ignorance as to how the American legal system works. That a person accused of a crime is innocent until proven guilty and is entitled to a fair trial before a jury of his or her peers is the anchor that makes America a great nation, with citizens who are free. American justice depends not only on fair and impartial prosecution of lawbreakers, but also includes the dedicated lawyers who are committed to providing the best defense possible that a defendant is guaranteed to receive. That was Dimitriou's specialty, and no one that knew him doubted his ethics, professionalism, and dedication.

When Manny Dimitriou died of cancer at age 74 there was no shortage of eulogies. It was mentioned that he was one of the acknowledged "legends" of the Berks County Bar.

He worked until he literally couldn't continue any longer. He died in Lancaster, Pennsylvania, on Saturday, March 15, 2008. He was taken from the courtroom the previous Monday and hospitalized. The presiding judge, Louis J. Farina, declared a mistrial after Dimitriou became too ill to continue.

Manny was involved in many notable, landmark, and high-profile cases. At the time of his death he was defending in Lancaster court, Warren Trent, 50, accused of shooting his former girlfriend Amy Lynn Matz in the back of the head in 2004. Their nine-year-old daughter Jacklyn Trent witnessed the killing.

In a 2007 trial, Manny defended Pottsville, Pennsylvania's BVM Nativity High School teacher, football and track coach Daniel M. Shields, 63. The longtime coach and teacher was charged with sexually assaulting a female student and secretly videotaping her and two other girls in a locker room.

Other cases included the 1974 defense of Stewart Cohen who was tried as a contract killer, James Eway's trial for the 1995 shooting death of Ephrata, Pennsylvania, teenager Michael Abate III, and the drug case against Doctor Patrick A. Mazza. Manny tried the first successful "battered woman syndrome" case in Pennsylvania when he won Audrey Moyer's acquittal of killing her husband Barry Moyer, and further established the double jeopardy rule in the 1968 trial of Peter T. Campana, charged with disorderly conduct, resisting arrest, and assault on a police officer.

He defended Michael Allen Slote, one of four men accused of first-degree murder in the 1982 slaying of reputed drug kingpin Richard Good. This case, which received the personal attention of then Pennsylvania attorney general LeRoy Zimmerman, was prosecuted by special prosecutor Richard Guida, made famous by prosecuting the 1979 Susan Reinert murder case.

Reinert was a teacher at Upper Merion High School in suburban Philadelphia. Her naked and bruised body was found stuffed in the trunk of her car in Harrisburg, Pennsylvania. Her two children were never found. Her coworkers Jay C. Smith and William Bradfield were tried and convicted of the crime.

In the 1980 Mazza case, 56-year-old Doctor Mazza, team physician for the Philadelphia Phillies' minor league club in Reading, was accused of illegally prescribing amphetamines for some Philadelphia Phillies players, including pitchers Steve Carlton, Larry Christenson, and Randy Lerch, and players Pete Rose, Greg Luzinski, Larry Bowa, and sportscaster and former catcher Tim McCarver. Doctor Mazza, along with Reading men Robert L. Masley, 46 at the time, and his son Robert M. Masley, 24 at the time, were accused of illegally obtaining the drugs at local pharmacies.

Dimitriou was hired to defend Mazza and the two Masleys. After all charges were dismissed, he said that his clients never would have been charged if the ballplayers would have admitted they accepted the drugs and used them for various aches and pains, weight control, fatigue, and the desperate need for more pep and energy.

Admittedly not good reasons—especially within a professional sport that is paranoid about drug use of any kind and enforces strict rules against its abuse—but reasons nevertheless that preclude criminal wrongdoing. Manny stated after the charges were dismissed, "What you have here are a bunch of ballplayers who are world champions, but who also are champions of lying."

One of Dimitriou's last cases was representing Berks County mortgage broker Wesley A. Snyder in federal court. Snyder had pleaded guilty of running a scheme that defrauded more that 800 clients and investors out of an estimated $29.2 million.

At the time of Manny's death he was representing former Lancaster County coroner G. Gary Kirchner, who was charged by the state attorney general's office with unlawful computer use and conspiracy for allegedly sharing his password to a secure law-enforcement Web site with Lancaster newspaper reporters.

Chapter 6

The Hearing

On July 29, 1981, before the start of the Gilmore preliminary hearing that had been moved to Sinking Spring, a neighboring town west of Muhlenberg, District Judge Henry Schultz released the 44-page statement that Doctor Gilmore had made to police and assistant district attorney on December 11, 1980.

Spearheading the prosecution was Charles Haddad, special prosecutor. Haddad's law practice was based in Wernersville, a small town located a few miles west of Sinking Spring.

First on Haddad's agenda was questioning Doctor John Keith—whose specialty was anatomical pathology—a pathologist employed on the staff of the Reading Hospital and Medical Center since May 1973. Haddad asked him what his duties were at the hospital. Keith responded, "I perform autopsies for the hospital and I perform surgical pathology and cytology."

Keith was on call on Thanksgiving Day—November 27, 1980. He explained that being on call meant he would be available in case any problem develops in the laboratory or if any physician at the hospital would want an autopsy on a deceased patient to be performed that day. "I'm also theoretically on call for consultation for any surgical problem that might arise in an emergency surgery and if a deceased person is brought to Reading Hospital and it is a coroner's case. It has been the habit of the acting coroner or deputy coroner, if he wants an autopsy, simply to call the pathologist who is on duty that day to do it." Keith had been assigned to that Thanksgiving Day for a long period of time by virtue of a rotating holiday duty schedule that was drawn up yearly.

Haddad asked, "Did you, on Thanksgiving Day of 1980, receive a call to perform an autopsy at the hospital?"

Keith verified, "Yes. I have a phone mate [answering machine] at home and I was absent in the morning and received a telephone message from Doctor George Kershner, who is a physician working in the emergency room at Reading Hospital. I believe his call came in on my phone mate around 10:00—I'm not certain exactly when since I wasn't there. He informed me that Patricia Gilmore had been brought to the hospital that morning dead on arrival, and that a full autopsy had been ordered by Doctor Glosser and that I was to get in contact with him as soon as possible." Kershner was a local product, a graduate of Albright College in Reading, and Philadelphia's Jefferson Medical College.

Keith then recalled that he called Kershner in the early afternoon simply to confirm what he had heard on his answering machine. As a result of that telephone conversation, Keith went to the hospital about 3:00 or 4:00 in the afternoon. The autopsy was performed, and was completed about 9:00 p.m.

Haddad wanted to know the sequence of events that happened after Keith got to the hospital, and asked Keith if he could recall the details.

"Yes, I went to the autopsy room and there waiting was Robert Durling. He is an assistant to us in the autopsy room. He is not—he has no medical degree of any sort but he is an autopsy room assistant. He was there and the body of Patricia Gilmore was there, and I performed an external examination and—."

Haddad interrupted and asked what he observed during the external examination.

"There were several features on external examination that I noted. One was the presence of certainly four and possibly five, and I must say that I cannot rule out more, needle marks on the right buttock. The exact measurements are in my report. I could refer to them if you wanted."

Haddad asked Keith to do so, and District Judge Schultz made sure that defense counsel Dimitriou also had a copy.

Haddad wanted to know if Keith took any clothing off the body when he conducted his visual examination.

"There was a pair of blue panties and I cannot specifically remember whether I removed them or whether they had been removed, but they were with the body and they were examined."

Keith continued to refer to his written report, in which he noted that there were five circular bloodstains—they were all smaller than a dime—more or less in a vertical line over the right midportion of the right buttock.

Haddad wanted to know if the bloodstains on the panty correlate in position/location to the needle marks observed on the body.

Keith said, "On the surface of the upper portion of the right buttock, to the right and left, one could see a slight indentation of the skin, and this corresponded with and could certainly have been caused and most probably was caused by the presence of an elastic band of panties themselves. The marks, the blood marks on the pants, I did not put the pants back on but simply stretching out the panties and looking at the buttock and looking at the panties, the blood marking corresponding very well lateral and vertical orientation with the needle puncture marks that I saw on the buttock."

Haddad wanted to know whether photos were taken of the buttock area. "Yes, I have lost the habit of taking photographs in the autopsy room due to the presence in our hospital of a very expert medical photographer, Ron Endy. He was not at the hospital that day being a vacation day. Mr. Durling assured me that he had the knack for taking the pictures. He went and got our laboratory camera and took pictures of the needle marks. What I don't—may I go on at this point?"

Haddad said, "Certainly."

"We ran out of film and I went out to try to find some more film. All the stores were closed. I went to a small nearby mini-market, was not able to find the right film and so, when I returned to the hospital, I actually called Mr. Endy and pleaded with him to come to the hospital in order to take these pictures which I thought were important."

Haddad wanted to know if all the photographs were taken in Doctor Keith's presence.

"The pictures taken by—all the pictures taken by Mr. Durling and all the pictures taken by Mr. Endy of Patricia Gilmore were in my presence and I cannot specifically remember whether or not the photographs of the buttock were taken by Mr. Durling or Mr. Endy, but they were taken by either one or the other and they were taken in my presence."

Haddad projected a picture on the screen in the courtroom and asked Keith if he could identify it. He described it as the surface of the skin on the buttock region and a piece of tape with her name and the date 11/27/80 printed on it. While looking at the projected picture he explained, "Here you see two needle puncture marks and here you see two needle puncture marks, and I am not certain but I believe that it is the third questionable needle mark in the first group that I described, that is possibly a second."

Haddad wanted to know what portion of the body was pictured. Keith explained that he was not 100 percent certain of the exact orientation in relation to the rest of the body because of the very isolated photographic picture, but because what appeared to be an indentation due to the elastic band from her panties, the needle marks pictured were below that line. At any rate, Keith reminded Haddad that the needle marks were described in the autopsy report.

Haddad asked, "Now in your report and from your visual observation, did you classify the groups in any way?" Keith acknowledged, "I have described them as two couplets that were in a more or less vertical alignment in respect to the body. These two certainly were themselves in an alignment. They were with slightly—these did not form a perfectly vertical line with the axis of the body. They were close enough so I simply used as an expression couplet and I believe that that is all the further that I went with the actual description of the needle marks."

Keith noted that at this time he had not yet done any cutting on the body and didn't notice anything else abnormal before he turned the body over to examine the anterior surface, including the face, her back, and buttocks. Because the body was lying face down, the blood settled in the subcutaneous tissue beneath the skin over the entire anterior surface of her body, including her face. Because the back of her head, back, and buttocks were now resting on the autopsy table, the blood from her face, as well as from the anterior chest region and anterior portion of her legs, drained away from underneath the skin so that the darkened color disappeared and the color of her normal body pigmentation returned.

Keith recalled that he noticed a definite raised, swollen, discolored bruise just beneath the right eye and just slightly lateral to the cheekbone. "There was a distinct, firm swelling with discoloration measuring, the firmest nucleus of center of the swelling, of at least two centimeters in diameter." He also noticed discoloration at the base of her nose on both sides of the nostrils, and the nose itself was bent slightly to the left.

As Haddad prepared to project another autopsy photograph on the courtroom screen, he was confronted with a situation that the defense was sure to take issue with. Keith described the makings of controversy. "I should say perhaps at this point, because of the interlude between when I ran out of film and when Mr. Endy appeared at the hospital to take pictures, and I—actually, the photograph that had actually been taken of the face and it turned out later that this particular photograph did not develop properly. That was the one that Mr. Durling took. Having thought that the photograph was already taken of the face and in order to fully document the age and nature of the lesion in that cheek region, I incised and took a piece of tissue for microscopy. The incision was subsequently sutured by Mr. Durling and the picture that we will see of her face was taken by Mr. Endy when he later arrived at the hospital, so that the actual incision and suture that we see here is my work; the swelling and discoloration was present before."

Haddad wanted to move past this possible complication of his case as fast as possible. He fired a direct question to Keith, "Can you describe to us the injuries you observed on that day, please?"

Keith referred to the compromised photograph, which not only showed the injuries he described being present on his initial examination, but now also the incisions he made without the proper photographic documentation. He noted that some blood shown was possibly due to the incision he had made when he opened the scalp posteriorally. He did not recall whether he had already examined the brain at that point. He pointed out the lesion and the swelling area that the picture was taken to illustrate. He showed the suture that he made in order to take a section of skin and underlying fat so that microscopy of the fresh hemorrhage and approximate age of that lesion could be made. "You will notice also that the light—it is not makeup—this is shiny through here, a definite distinct bluish coloration in this region that was present before this incision was made. The incision itself in the post mortem tissue does not at the time account for any discoloration of the skin itself." He explained that a second lesion in the face region, quite close to the other lesion, was hemorrhage, not mascara—it was a distinct subcutaneous hemorrhage involving a little bit less than the inner or center half of the lower eyelid.

Haddad wanted to know which eye Keith was referring to. He said it was the right eye. "This lesion here specifically is what in common parlance is known as a black eye." He noted that even though it's a bit more difficult to notice, there is apparent bluish, reddish discoloration around the right side of the nose.

"Doctor, you also indicated that there was bruising to the left side of the nose?" Keith confirmed, "Yes. It's more pronounced on the left side. There was no question about it. Again, you have this bluish discoloration here more or less on the top of the wing of the left nostril but extending down to the base region. Again here—this is again—there is no actual rupture of the skin surface although from the appearance of this and, as I remember it, it was distinctly possible that there were very small microhemorrhages just beneath the skin surface in more or less a linear fashion right here or a linear pattern right at this point [*indicating*]. Here again you can see distinctly the subcutaneous hemorrhage in the right lower eyelid."

Haddad asked if Keith's visual examination continued to other parts of the body including the hand. Keith recalled that he did photograph a reddish bruised area over the left wrist just at the base of the thumb.

Keith acknowledged that he performed a complete autopsy for the purpose of discovering an explanation for the cause of death, explaining that the esophagus is routinely examined in every autopsy, as is the larynx that constitutes the upper respiratory tract. He noted that he found a very small amount of vomit in the esophagus.

Haddad asked, "Was the amount of vomitus which you found in the esophagus of the decedent sufficient in amount to cause her death by asphyxiation?" Keith answered, "No. To be more precise at this point, food in the esophagus would not cause asphyxiation because that constitutes the upper portion of the digestive tract. It does not interfere with the breathing. There was a small amount of vomitus in the larynx extending in—a very small amount extending up into the posterior oral cavity. This constituted a layer, a very thin layer of—recognized as vomitus but, in my opinion, could not have obstructed the airway or caused asphyxiation. There was also a small amount, a very small amount of vomitus just below the larynx, the upper respiratory tract. Again, if I were to—if all of that vomitus material were to be collected and weighed, I would have to say that maximum weight would have to be an ounce or less."

He also mentioned that during the autopsy urine was saved for drug screening, and that the liver appeared grossly congested, and part of it was frozen in the event of future toxicology, as well as a portion of one of the kidneys, which appeared normal. He also stated that there was minimum to light atherosclerosis present, and a very, very minimal amount of what is called endometriosis on the surface of the uterus, which should be considered as an incidental, insignificant finding. Endometriosis is a female health disorder that occurs when cells from the lining of the womb (uterus) grow in other areas of the body. This can lead to pain, irregular bleeding, and problems getting pregnant (infertility).

Haddad asked a critical question, very important to the prosecution of the case. "Now, so far as any of the organs and body systems which you examined, were any of them in a condition which would have been the cause of death for Patricia Gilmore?" Keith affirmed, "From a gross examination, I would have to say that nothing was found of all the findings that I have recorded so far, the gross findings could not explain death."

At this time Keith presented a detailed, graphic description of his examination of the brain after Haddad inquired whether the doctor noticed anything out of the ordinary. "In reflecting back the scalp; this is to say, in reflecting forward the scalp and examining the undersurface of the scalp, a fresh bruise was noted in the scalp and its location accorded to an area just left of the midline of the head and slightly above the level of the left eyebrow. A photograph was taken of this, I believe."

Haddad asked if there were any other injuries observed in the scalp examination. "Yes. There was a similar fresh hemorrhagic bruise of the scalp, more or less it's similarly located over the back region of the head. In purely anatomical terms, it is located over the center portion of the occipital bone."

Keith was questioned as to whether he telephoned Gilmore after he discovered the facial and head injuries. He didn't remember whether he talked to Gilmore before performing the autopsy, but did recall talking to him twice, once during the early stage of the autopsy when he asked him several questions, and then after the autopsy was completed telling him briefly what he had found. "I specifically remember asking Doctor Gilmore both about the needle marks and the bruise on the right side of the face that is just below the right eye. I do not remember whether or not I mentioned to him or asked him about the other two bruises described that I saw in the scalp."

Of course Haddad was interested in knowing Gilmore's reply to Keith's questions regarding those two areas. All he got was Keith recalling that Gilmore didn't understand how the needle marks or the bruising got there.

Keith took blood from the right chamber of the heart just after opening the body to obtain a blood sample for alcohol determination and another for drug evaluation. He then carefully removed the skin and underlying fat that had the needle marks in anticipation of possible toxicological studies of these tissues to determine what substances might have been injected in these clearly recognizable needle mark sites. Keith later turned over all these samples to Muhlenberg Police Detective Hadley.

Because the autopsy wasn't completed until about 9 p.m. that evening, the laboratory tests weren't performed until the next day. Keith telephoned Glosser and told him that the cause of death should be listed as toxicology pending. This ruling simply meant that toxicological studies are to be undertaken, and the results have not yet been obtained. It implies that there is the possibility that the cause of death can be ascribed to toxicological reasons.

Keith gave Glosser the preliminary findings of the autopsy, including the bruising and the volume of vomit. He did not specify at this point the findings of the needle marks on the buttock since their discovery deviated from normal autopsy findings. Keith did not conclude at that time what caused the death of Patricia Gilmore.

The laboratory results showed that Patty Gilmore had 0.24 grams per deciliter of alcohol in her blood—she was obviously intoxicated. The legal limit for intoxication for the Pennsylvania Bureau of Traffic Control is 0.10 grams per deciliter. Keith did not consider this level of alcohol to be adequate to have accounted for the death of a young, apparently healthy woman in her thirties.

The urine screen for drugs, performed at the Reading Hospital, showed an extremely high concentration of meperidine, commonly known by its brand name Demerol. That urine test was not acceptable in a court of law—it could only be used as a guideline. This high concentration of meperidine required sending a blood sample to a specialized laboratory for specific measurements of all drugs in the blood, including meperidine.

Keith noted, "I informed Doctor Glosser that my next step would then be to send the blood to a laboratory for quantification of it; that is to say, the exact measurement of the exact level of the concentration of Demerol in the blood."

On the following Monday, December 1, Keith sent blood samples to National Medical Services, whose laboratory eventually completed the blood's analysis. Keith couldn't recall the exact date the quantitative analysis results were reported back to him, but did remember that the report was dated December 10. He also didn't remember whether he had gotten a phone call from Doctor Cohn or whether he simply got a printed report one or two days later.

The report stated that the serum Demerol level was 2.9 micrograms per milliliter of serum, and they indicated in their report that this was consistent with acute meperidine intoxication. The report also mentioned that no other controlled drugs or abuse was detected, and there was a presumption that the laboratory performed a screen appropriate to the substance submitted.

Haddad then asked a crucial question. "Now, as a result of the test results you received from National Medical Services, did you reach a conclusion as to the cause of death of Patricia Gilmore?"

Doctor Keith responded, "Yes. At the time that I received these results, these are the first toxicological reports that I received from the National Medical laboratories. I concluded that we now had a cause of death and I specifically wrote that cause of death at this time and communicated it by telephone to Doctor Glosser, that the cause of death was acute poisoning (narcosis) by alcohol (0.24 grams per deciliter) and meperidine (2.9 micrograms per milliliter); that is to say, that I felt that the cause of death was a narcotic poisoning due to alcohol and meperidine, both of which had high levels in the serum of this patient."

Haddad asked Keith to explain how the meperidine and alcohol can cause death in an individual. Keith said that both alcohol and meperidine have markedly depressant effects on the central nervous system and specifically on the cardiorespiratory centers of the central nervous system located in the brain stem—they will depress the function of the heart and the function of the breathing centers so that they can, alone or in combination when they are in high levels, cause the blood to be denied an adequate amount of oxygen due to shallow and slow breathing, and they can produce a decreased heart rhythm and weak heartbeat. Keith stressed that these circumstances are carried to extreme when one or both of these functions stop simultaneously.

Haddad asked, "Are you stating, Doctor, that it is your conclusion that this is what caused the death of Patricia Gilmore?"

Keith confirmed, "Yes. The additional microscopic finding that I found in this case was edema of the lungs. This was found in more than one of microscopic sections taken from various regions of both lungs."

Haddad wanted to know what edema was. Keith explained that edema is fluid from the blood, but containing no red blood cells, that appears in the air spaces of the lining where the normal gas exchanges take place. Keith said it is a finding seen in people with heart failure, and in this particular case he considered it a finding of acute heart failure.

Keith said that Patricia Gilmore's heart failure was caused by the combination of the alcohol and meperidine. He said that her coronary arteries were in good condition and samples of her heart muscle showed the heart was normal.

At this time Haddad returned to the subject of the injuries that were discovered on the body.

"Doctor, I would like to go back, please, to the facial and injuries to the scalp. Is it possible that the injuries which you noted, both by visual observation and also through bisection, could have occurred after the death of Patricia Gilmore?"

Keith replied emphatically, "No, it's impossible for these to have occurred after death." He further explained, "The gross findings of the swelling—there is no way that the swelling can occur as a post mortem injury. The swelling of the soft tissues—that is to say, the subcutaneous fat in the region of the cheek where the lesion was present—this was noted as a gross finding. It was also noted—edema and fresh hemorrhage into this fatty tissue was noted on microscopic examination. These findings would not be present from a post mortem injury. The whole—this statement also applies to the hemorrhage that I noted in the scalp, both—in both lesions over the left eyebrow and over the posterior portion of the head."

Haddad brought up the fact that Keith's conclusion was that the combination of meperidine and alcohol was sufficient in quantity to cause death, and that he relied partly on the information received from Doctor Rieders and Doctor Cohn from National Medical Services.

Keith recalled that he had had several conversations with Doctor Cohn and one conversation with Doctor Rieders. The conversations with Doctor Cohn were by telephone during December, January, February, and possibly March. These conversations were in the course and in combination with the reporting of National Medical Services' toxicological findings, both from serum samples and secondly from the subcutaneous tissue from the buttock, along with toxicological findings of the blood, urine, vomitus, liver, and kidney.

Haddad asked about Keith's professional opinion as to how Patricia Gilmore sustained the injuries that left the marks on her body.

"The injuries were, first of all I should say not caused by a sharp instrument because no cutting of the skin itself, other than over the cheek region or the head lesions that I previously described were noted. They were caused by what can be described as blunt injury, blunt trauma, due to a hard blow by either a blunt—by a blunt instrument which, of course, can cover many different objects or many different types of hitting or blows."

Keith confirmed that the injuries he saw on the body were consistent with receiving the injuries by a strike from another human being; especially the injury to the face, beneath the eye, and the eyelid would be easily possible from a fist. He said that the injuries to the scalp could be due to a blow either received from falling on a firm object, possibly wooden—not carpet, but firmer than that—either from falling or from receiving them from a wooden object.

He was precise about at least two blows received by the

head, one in the back and one in the front, and that the blows were different from the injury on the right side of the face underneath the eye. He also had difficulty trying to decide how the injuries to the left side of the nose were received. He felt that how that injury was received should be deferred to a forensic pathologist.

At this point in the questioning, defense counsel Manny Dimitriou sought to review the details of Keith's arriving at the hospital to perform the autopsy. Keith confirmed that he resided in suburban Ruscombmanor Township, about 8 to 10 miles from the hospital. He repeated that he got the phone message from Kershner that a woman had arrived DOA at the hospital. When he returned Kershner's phone call he spoke briefly to Kershner and got some information, specifically that the name of the deceased woman was Patricia Gilmore, and that she was the wife of Doctor Irvin Gilmore. Kershner also told him that she was found dead in the Gilmores' bed that morning and that she was brought to the hospital by the Muhlenberg Ambulance. Kershner seemed to recall that the ambulance was accompanied by a Muhlenberg patrolman.

Keith responded to Dimitriou's wanting to know more about the fresh needle marks. Dimitriou said he wasn't certain whether Kershner had said during the phone conversation that fresh needle marks on her right buttock were discovered in the hospital emergency room.

Dimitriou asked, "You are not sure about that?" Keith responded, "I'm sure about that."

Dimitriou wanted to know if Keith talked to Kershner in person before he began the autopsy. Keith said, "I believe that I only saw Doctor Kershner in person once and that was after I had in fact examined the organs, the thoracic as well as the abdominal cavities as well as the brain. I do not think that I talked to him again on the telephone in the hospital, although I am not certain. It is possible that he might remember. I cannot specifically remember if I did talk to him again. I cannot think of any other information which he gave me that was of any more importance or help in doing my autopsy."

Dimitriou asked if Keith had talked to anyone else before he began the autopsy. Keith said he talked to Glosser before the autopsy. "Who ordered you to do the autopsy?" Keith said, "I was notified by Doctor Kershner that the coroner, and I believe he said Doctor Glosser, had ordered a full autopsy."

Dimitriou asked, "Is this something that he told you when you spoke to him?" Keith replied that he was told a full autopsy was to be performed and that the coroner ordered it. "This, I might add, is a very habitual way that we often do autopsies. More often than not, we do not personally go to the coroner before beginning an autopsy, although in this case we did."

Dimitriou recapped what Keith had just recalled. "So first you got a call from Doctor Kershner, who notified you that the coroner had ordered the autopsy. Then you in fact did talk to Doctor Glosser?" Keith confirmed that he talked to Glosser before he started the autopsy.

Keith then offered that he was not certain whether he spoke to Gilmore before the autopsy began. He said he was certain he spoke to Gilmore twice that evening, once after the autopsy was complete and very possibly spoke to him the first time before performing the autopsy.

Dimitriou's method of operating was to carefully comb through the details of all the testimony given, making sure that a witness's story held up consistently. He made no exception to this rule while questioning Doctor Keith.

He asked, "Now, when you first saw Patricia Gilmore, was she in the autopsy room?" Keith confirmed that was true. When questioned further, he said Robert Durling was present, and that Patricia Gilmore's body was brought to the hospital on November 27 at about 9:30 a.m., approximately six hours before Keith came and saw her.

Dimitriou asked, "Five or six, okay. Now, do you know who else had contact with Patricia Gilmore of your own knowledge?" Keith said he wasn't certain if he understood the question. He said he didn't know how many people saw her in the emergency room, but he did know that Kershner saw her, and Durling was with the body in the autopsy room.

Dimitriou asked, "Okay. And how about transporting?" Keith said, "When she was brought to the autopsy room, no one else would have seen her. She would have been put—we have refrigerated compartments, she would have been put in the refrigerated compartment and the autopsy room would be locked with the alarm set."

Dimitriou had questions about the layout of the autopsy room and the configuration of the stainless steel autopsy table, and got confirmation that the body was lying on this table when Keith arrived. "And I believe you testified yesterday on direct examination that she was lying face down; is that correct?"

"I'm not certain if I testified that when I came in the room she was lying face down. I know that the first part of my external examination was performed on her lying face down, and I cannot specifically remember whether or not that involved turning her over, and I would assume, from autopsies that I know about, how we originally do autopsies, that this would be the way that this would have been done. I would have entered the room, she would have been lying face up on the table and when we decided to examine her posterior surface, we would turn her over. It is generally, almost—well, it's an unwritten, unspoken and it's a rule that deceased bodies, that they are lying on autopsy tables unattended are lying on their backs."

Dimitriou persisted. "But in this particular case, you are not absolutely certain whether she was in fact face down when you entered the room?"

Keith answered, "I can say that I can never remember an autopsy that I have ever performed at the Reading Hospital where I have walked into the autopsy room and the body had been placed on the autopsy table by one of the two of our assistants face down. It is simply a practice that is never—that is just not used."

Dimitriou then reviewed with Keith the events that took place before and during the autopsy. Keith said he didn't know how long the body was on the autopsy table before he arrived, noting that Durling would be the person who would know that. He explained that he performed an extensive external examination of the body necessary before actually performing the autopsy. After doing this examination he went to an early supper in the hospital and then took about ten minutes to drive to a nearby convenience store to buy the needed film. Dimitriou pointed out that taking this time accounts somewhat for the length of time that was involved for this particular autopsy.

Keith said, "Yes, that accounts for a portion." He continued, "Yes, I spent more time on this autopsy certainly than I usually do on an autopsy."

He spoke about how Patricia Gilmore's lungs were heavily congested. He stated that the heart appeared normal for a relatively young person's, and there was an almost total absence of atherosclerosis, described in his testimony as typically mild for a person of Patricia Gilmore's age.

Dimitriou asked, "Now, Doctor Keith, you also indicated that you took two blood specimens from the right heart, is that correct; one for alcohol and one for drugs?" Keith said that was correct and the blood specimens were properly labeled with the name of the patient and the date, and they were taken by him personally to a laboratory refrigerator in the hospital and locked in a cabinet. Keith said he did this after finishing the autopsy at approximately 9 p.m., about the same time he spoke with Gilmore and Glosser the last time.

Dimitriou asked, "Did you have any further contact with those blood samples?" Keith replied that yes he did, but not with both blood samples—the next morning the blood for the alcohol was removed by the technician, and that he wasn't present when that happened.

Dimitriou said, "Well then, you didn't have any further contact with that one container that had the blood for the blood alcohol; is that correct?" Keith responded, "Right, correct."

Dimitriou's obvious next question was, "When was the next time that you had any contact with the container that was containing the blood for the drug samples?"

Keith responded; "That same day, Friday, that is to say, the day after the autopsy, I would—I am assuming now that it must have been about midday or early in the afternoon. After I had received information from Esther Bell, the lab technician, that the Demerol concentration in the urine was highly concentrated or was of a high number, it was at that time that I called Doctor Glosser to inform him of this and to inform him that a specific quantitative measurement in the serum of Demerol should be made, and that this—in order for this to be done, the specimen would have to be sent out of the laboratory. The response at this time of Doctor Glosser was not confirmatory of this proposal.

"After that phone conversation, I was then faced with the dilemma of what to do with this specimen, so I retrieved the specimen from the refrigerator and took it to the autopsy room, which is locked at all times, and put it in the freezer in the autopsy room, so that was my second contact with that specimen."

Dimitriou wanted to know if Keith retrieved the specimen after his phone conversation with Glosser. Keith replied that he had, and that he placed the specimen in the freezer early Friday afternoon.

Dimitriou asked, "Is the freezer locked?" Keith replied, "The autopsy room is locked, not the freezer."

The following Monday Keith went and retrieved the sample, confirming later that it was exactly where he had placed it before, and was of the exact same appearance, including the height of the fluid in the container, his writing on the container, and the stopper still in it. He took the container to laboratory manager Mel Weaver and instructed him to send the specimen to the Upjohn Laboratory for quantification of Demerol and additional drug screening, noting that the urine was positive for meperidine and that the blood-alcohol reading was 0.24.

Weaver packaged the specimen, and the courier for Upjohn Laboratories picked it up. Keith said that was the last time he saw the specimen.

Dimitriou inquired about the detailed procedures for handling all laboratory specimens. Keith explained that he didn't know what the procedures were, but he did know that Weaver followed approved procedures. Dimitriou reacted, "I see. You assume?" Keith persisted, "Yes, I'm assuming."

Dimitriou asked, "Now between Friday and Monday, of

course, there are other people that have access to this locked autopsy room?" Keith replied, "No." Dimitriou responded, "Were you the only one that has a key to that room?" Keith said, "No, I don't know all of the keys—everyone that has keys to that. That would be a piece of information that could be supplied, although I simply don't know."

Dimitriou persisted, "My question simply is that there are other people who have keys to the autopsy room who would have access to it; isn't that a fact?" Keith said he couldn't think of other people; he did say that Mr. Durling had a key, and conceded there is a restricted number of people, but he didn't know how many.

Dimitriou was creating doubt—that was his primary strategy all along. "You would have no way of knowing whether anyone had entered that room between Friday and Monday; isn't that right?" Keith was forced to answer, "No, I would not have any way of knowing for sure." After Keith pointed out that the door is always locked and there is an alarm system, Dimitriou responded, "If you don't mind, Doctor Keith, just answer my questions."

Dimitriou said that Haddad could ask for any elaborations later, but right now he wanted to know what Keith's experience was with the drug meperidine. Keith explained that he had very little experience, and that he could not remember ever having done an autopsy in which such a high concentration of meperidine was a factor in the final autopsy report. Dimitriou wanted to know if he was familiar with the therapeutic, toxic, and fatal levels of meperidine, and the ranges of levels.

Keith restated, "I'm not—I was not familiar at all when I did this autopsy. Since that time, I have seen papers where reports are given about toxicological data on this and other drugs.

So that my information is information that I have encountered in scientific literature since the time of this autopsy."

Dimitriou inquired, "By the way, other than what you sent to Rieders in the way of the organs such as liver, kidney, et cetera—were any of those pieces of organs saved for further study?"

Keith recalled that he sent a portion of the kidney to be analyzed for toxicology, and took a section for microscopic examination. He said he sent a piece of liver for toxicological examination but didn't save any vomitus or other gastric contents that were sent to the laboratory, because normally microscopic examination isn't performed on gastric contents.

Dimitriou wanted to know about the tissue taken from the buttocks. Keith testified, "I took a section of that for my microscopic examination, and I have since been assured by Doctor Rieders that any more of the tissue which he still has, that I would like to do microscopic examination on."

Dimitriou asked, "How many autopsies have you performed where an overdose of other drugs, aside from meperidine, has been ascribed as the cause of death?" Keith said he couldn't be certain, but he supposed thirty would be a conservative estimate; and responding to Dimitriou's question as to how many he had performed on a drug addict, he said fewer than ten.

Dimitriou wanted to know if the doctor was familiar with the interaction between meperidine and alcohol. Keith replied, "I did not know—I have not read extensively in medical literature on the subject, but I—but I do know that the two effects—the effects of both of the substances are in many ways similar; that is, their effects on the central nervous system are in many ways very similar."

Dimitriou asked what the interaction is between meperidine and Lomotil. Keith confirmed that the cardiac and central nervous system effects are for the most part similar.

He was questioned whether he was familiar with the drug called Stadol. Keith said that was the name given to him during the autopsy, but he didn't examine further about the drug because he didn't get any information about its presence.

Keith confirmed during further questioning that Demerol is a synthetic opiate derivative, that he didn't know at what rate it metabolizes or eliminates in the body before death. Dimitriou asked, "Can you determine, from your observation, visual observation, how many times a particular drug, whether it be Demerol or anything else, was injected into the body?"

Keith responded, "That would be—that would depend on the findings at autopsy. If, to use an illustrative example, one had three or four clear needle marks on various portions of the fatty portion of the body, in a case of that sort it would be possible to remove the skin and underlying subcutaneous tissue from each of these injection sites and perform analysis of the concentration of the drug in question in that tissue, compare it to blood levels of that particular substance and if there was a wide discrepancy in favor of high concentration in the subcutaneous tissue, then I think the conclusion could be that in every one of the specimens where the concentration was much higher than in the blood, one can say that that was in conjunction with the finding of a needle mark, a site of injection of that particular drug."

Keith continued, "In this particular case, the determination of exactly how many times the drug in question, which is Demerol, was injected was complicated by the fact that, as you saw in the picture, the two groups of two needle marks, each were very close together, so close together, I believe that to have tried to remove the underlying tissue and separate them off according to the tracks of the new needles, and then determine the concentration in the fat of each of those separate specimens would have been impossible. Besides that, I did not feel that to specifically determine that was that necessary.

"So what I did was to remove the tissue and the skin surrounding each group of needle marks separately because they were, in themselves, far enough apart and submitted them as what you might call a coupled specimen since you are talking about two needle marks, at least in each of the specimens. I think, frankly, that this would be as far as it would be possible to go in deciding about the injection of meperidine in both of these sites; whether or not one could say from any particular procedure after that that each of these two needle marks in each of the two groups was the site of the injection of meperidine, might not be possible to determine."

Now Dimitriou drove home his point: "So that in summary in this particular case, you could not determine how many injections in fact there were of Demerol or any other drug, correct?"

Keith conceded this fact while recognizing it all depended to what extent one really felt it was important to know.

Dimitriou wanted to know in this particular case if that could be determined. Keith explained that it was possible to determine with additional work such as taking photographs and then extensively identifying and analyzing all the fatty specimens. If finding that they contained high concentrations of Demerol, he could conclude that both of these needle marks in that particular specimen received a Demerol injection.

Dimitriou asked, "You are saying you can do that now?"

Keith replied, "Yes, it would be possible in this particular case. I think that all of the data and photographs and information are available to make that verification."

Dimitriou continued his intense questioning. He now wanted to know whether the meperidine was injected at the same time or at different times. Keith said that to answer that question he would need to defer to a toxicologist, also what the time lapse was between the time of injection and the time of death. He explained that in theory these questions and answers are all related to the quantity of the dose and the strength of the dose. "What I mean by dose, I am talking about the total amount of Demerol. I couldn't care whether the concentration is lower or higher, if you are going into the subcutaneous tissue or into the skin, it doesn't really matter. It's going to be absorbed rapidly and it's really the total amount that is important. As far as the concentration goes, I think that there are, generally speaking, standard concentrations."

Dimitriou persisted, asking how much time would have lapsed between the time of the injection and the time of death. Keith again stated that to answer that question he would have to defer to a toxicologist.

Dimitriou, reminding Keith that he had described the needle marks as "fresh," wanted to know what he defined as "fresh." Keith explained that referring to the marks as "fresh" is based on the gross appearance of the needle marks from the skin surface, where there was a small amount of crusted blood on the top, the appearance of the subcutaneous fat, and on the microscopic examination of the fatty tissue taken from one of the needle tracks. "Based on my observation of all three of these parameters, I would consider these needle marks and the underlying hemorrhage from the needle tracks to have occurred less than, within about six hours or less of the time of death."

Patricia Wolfe
Senior Class Picture, Muhlenberg Township High School 1962.

May Queen Court – *Muhlenberg Township High School 1962.*
Patricia Wolfe is 4th female student from top (marked with arrow).

Doctor Irvin Gilmore

Emmanuel "Manny" Dimitriou
Prominent defense attorney

Front of the Gilmore House along Kutztown Road.
Police and the ambulance parked here when they arrived.

Side view of the Gilmore House.
Notice the garage and beach house surrounding the swimming pool.

This cottage in the Cherokee Ranch section of Muhlenberg was the location of Doctor Gilmore's medical practice.

Chapter 7

The Emergency Room Doctor

As the preliminary hearing continued, Haddad next questioned Doctor George Kershner, who was on duty in the emergency room that Thanksgiving morning. Kershner stated that he left the emergency room and went back to the room that the body had been placed in and, after a brief examination, pronounced her dead. He then called the coroner and notified him of the death and gave a brief description of the body. The coroner ordered an autopsy.

Kershner said he noticed the body had developed a substantial amount of rigor mortis, the anterior or front portion of the body was deeply purple, and there were some bloodstains on the right rear panties. The obvious assumption was that Patricia Gilmore died in the prone position, gravity having pulled edema or cellular fluid and liquid and blood with it anteriorly.

Haddad asked, "Did you conduct any further visual examination in regard to the bloodstains on the panties?"

Kershner answered, "Yes, sir. I lowered the panties and there were—I don't recall the number—there were two sets of needle marks or puncture wounds." Doctor Kershner explained that he noticed the wounds were on the buttock underneath the bloodstained area. Later in the morning after the body was turned over, Kershner still didn't notice any bruises because the blood hadn't drained to the rear of the body; that can take several hours.

By late afternoon or early evening Doctor Kershner observed the body again, however this time it was lying on its back and the purple discoloration of the front of the body had now shifted to the rear. At this time Kershner noticed a bruise somewhere in the area of the right eye. He stated that he believed it was below the eye, but didn't recall that for a fact.

Haddad asked, "And you are saying you did not observe

that same bruise when it was brought into your room, in the emergency room?"

Kershner said, "It would have been impossible because the discoloration had changed because of the position."

Dimitriou began his questioning of Doctor Kershner. "Had you had any telephone calls from anyone about Patricia Gilmore's body being brought to the Reading Hospital?" Kershner replied that he had around 8:30 a.m. "And from whom did you receive this call?" Kershner replied that the call was from Doctor Gilmore.

"He said that he had just awakened and found his wife dead in bed next to him."

Doctor Kershner couldn't remember whether Gilmore brought up about an autopsy being necessary. Kershner remembered someone talking to him about it, but he wasn't sure whether it was Gilmore.

Dimitriou asked, "So that I understand your testimony, Doctor Kershner, are you saying that you have a recollection that someone told you that a post would be needed?"

Kershner replied, "As you say that, I vaguely recall someone saying that to me. I honestly say I don't remember who said it."

"And then you called Doctor Glosser, the coroner?"

Kershner replied, "That's correct."

Dimitriou asked, "When you saw it later in the afternoon at 3:30 or 4:00 or, I mean later in the afternoon or early evening, you noticed a bruise somewhere in the cheek area?" Kershner said that is correct, and that it wasn't the only observation he made.

"No, I think, as I recall, most of the autopsy was done, I did notice the hemorrhage in the scalp in the inside between the scalp and the skull and the needle punctures again."

"So you are saying the autopsy was already in progress when you arrived?" Kershner replied, "That is correct."

Dimitriou asked, "And you have given the response that the reason you didn't, or at least in your opinion that you didn't observe this bruise in the morning, was because of the color of the skin; is that correct?" Kershner replied, "That's correct."

"Did the police officer make any statements to you? Do you remember the police officer being there?" Kershner replied, "Yes, I do. They came, the one that—I don't recall which officer it was—one officer had an empty hypodermic syringe of something with him. I never touched it or looked at it that close. He produced it from his pocket and, to be perfectly frank, we tend to ignore a lot of things that police and ambulance people tell us because we are busy and in and out and so forth, and I didn't really pay much mind to what he said, but I recall him pulling out this thing from his pocket, I believe, and then put it back in."

Dimitriou asked, "Do you recall any other conversation between you and another one of the police officers?" Kershner responded, "I don't recall any, no."

"No, when you saw this bruise on the cheek or cheekbone later that afternoon, had the incision been made on that cheekbone yet?" Kershner replied that the autopsy was in fact in progress but the incision on the cheekbone had not yet been made.

Dimitriou wanted to know, "How would you describe this bruise that you observed?" Kershner replied, "It looked like a reasonably fresh black-and-blue mark."

"Would you classify it as a severe bruise or a very mild, slight bruise or what?"

Kershner said, "I don't think it was a very severe bruise, no. I would consider it a mild, a mild bruise-type thing."

Dimitriou had some more questions for Doctor Keith primarily concerning the needle marks—that both groupings, in Keith's opinion, were made approximately six hours or less from the time of death. Keith stated that he did not establish a specific time of death, but could put the time of death at approximately ten hours before he saw her body at three o'clock in the afternoon. He said, "But that, I must say, is plus or minus, plus or minus six hours; that is to say, anywhere from four to sixteen hours."

Dimitriou asked on what he based this opinion.

Keith explained, "That opinion is based on the fact that a fixed livor mortis was not present, and I would have expected—I must say that from the history and from documentation, I know that she was dead sometime before 9:00 that morning since she arrived DOA at the hospital. When one wouldn't ordinarily expect a fixed livor mortis by sixteen hours, one would expect certainly—now, that is to say if the deceased had died sixteen hours previous to when she was seen, there should be a fixed livor mortis and there was not."

Dimitriou said, "So that sixteen hours prior to that was about 11:00 p.m. on the twenty-sixth?"

Keith confirmed, "Yes; that is to say, that if she did have a fixed livor mortis, she should have been—that is to say, the fact that she did not have a fixed livor mortis, that allows me to say she was not dead for more that sixteen hours."

Keith's testimony thus indicated that death could have occurred anywhere from four to sixteen hours before the time that he saw the body at approximately 3:00 in the afternoon, in effect giving a range that corresponds anywhere from 11:00 or 12:00 at night to the next morning at 8:00 on the twenty-seventh.

Dimitriou asked, "And your testimony is that the needle marks would have been made anywhere from up to six hours prior to the time of death, whatever time that was?" Keith confirmed that as correct.

Then Dimitriou, referring in detail to autopsy photographs, grilled Doctor Keith again about the needle marks, primarily their placement. He wanted to confirm that Keith had stated previously that in addition to the two sets of needle marks, there were other needle marks.

Keith said he never said that.

Dimitriou asked, "I believe you testified that you found the presence of four or five needle marks in the right buttock and maybe more, two or three?"

Keith said, "No, I think I said four, possibly five and maybe more that were all in—they were present. They were all in that same region."

Dimitriou said, "You said maybe more?"

Keith responded, "I said maybe more, yes. I cannot confirm but they were not elsewhere on the body. If they were present at all, they were here."

Dimitriou didn't let up. "So that there is a possibility that there were more needle marks?"

Keith replied, "Yes. This was my impression at the time of the autopsy. The photograph seems to contradict that impression." He responded to Dimitriou's questioning about whether he noticed any old needle marks during the autopsy. Keith explained that he would not have been able to identify them, stating occasionally, a large intramuscular penicillin injection in the buttocks can cause what is called an aseptic abscess, but in general, needle marks of that size going in the buttocks after a period of a week would be totally undetectable.

Dimitriou kept the pressure on by intensifying his questioning. " Now, you indicated, Doctor Keith, in your autopsy report that two of the needle marks, an examination of those two indicated that the trajectory was cephalic or cephalad? What does that mean?"

Keith responded, "It means toward the head."

Dimitriou followed up, "So that the injection would have been made in an upward manner—is that correct?" The implication was that the needle entered and had been injected toward the head.

Dimitriou asked, "Could you tell me what that trajectory was?"

Doctor Keith replied, "No, I couldn't, I couldn't tell you that. That would be—I think it would—it would be a falsely accurate thing to say, because the buttock itself is curved so when you are talking about the axis of the body, it's different than the plane of the—plane—of the plane surface of the buttock which is in a constant state of curvature depending on where you are on it, so I feel that to give it—to try to give an exact measurement of that, although I could give you or may try to do it at the autopsy, I still think it would be more misinformative than informative."

Dimitriou stated, "In any event, it was your determination and opinion or finding that in those two needle marks, the trajectory was cephalic?"

Doctor Keith replied, "Yes."

Dimitriou wanted to know which two needle marks Keith was referring to.

Keith said, "They were not both in the same group. They are one in each group and I couldn't tell you which one in either group."

Dimitriou wanted a definite confirmation. "In other words,

you are saying that in the two that you did track the trajectory—one came from each of the two groups?"

Keith gave him the yes answer he wanted.

Dimitriou then asked more questions about the bruises to the back of the head, and the one that was on the forehead over the left eye. He asked if they were both consistent with falling.

Keith answered, "They would have been consistent with a falling, but I was careful to point out that one fall cannot have produced both since one was on one side of the head and one on the other."

Dimitriou replied, "I agree. But in any event, both the one in the front and the one in the back were consistent and could have been caused by a fall?"

Keith responded, "Yes."

Dimitriou asked about the bruise on the face, discoloration of the cheekbone and swelling, and that this would have been consistent with a blow from a fist.

Keith added, "Or any other object that was not sharp or markedly rough surfaced, because there was absolutely no abrasion of the skin itself."

Dimitriou confirmed that there was no concussion, no fracture, and that Keith reported earlier that he noticed no damage to the brain when it was examined.

Then he asked, "Now, isn't it a fair statement, Doctor Keith, that the bruise that you found on the cheekbone could be and would be consistent with a bump or a fall?"

Keith gave a detailed reply; "If the fall were on a—I tend to doubt that it's consistent with a fall because of where its location was here, and then there was an additional injury to the medial portion of the eye [indicating], where if you are talking about—if it were—if the person were to have fallen on an irregularly shaped object with some surface that would have allowed penetration into the eye socket, and that that object was smooth surfaced, then under those circumstances it's consistent."

Dimitriou asked, "Or a bump, if they bumped their face on the wall?"

Keith replied, "On a wall, I don't think it would have produced this lesion. I do not think a bump on the wall would have produced the hemorrhage in the inner aspect of the eyelid."

Dimitriou asked, "Now is it a fair statement, Doctor, that what you are testifying to now is to some degree a guess? You can't rule out the fact that these injuries could have been caused by a fall or a bump, can you?"

Keith said, "Well, these injuries could not have been caused by one fall."

Dimitriou said, "Fine. I am just simply saying, you cannot rule out the fact that these injuries to the face that you have described on the cheek and under the eyelid could have been caused by a fall?"

Keith admitted, "I can't rule it out."

Dimitriou asked, "All right. Isn't it a fact, Doctor Keith, that the statement that you made yesterday that it is impossible for bruises to occur after death is not entirely correct?"

Keith said, "The bruise, as I am describing it, being a lesion of it; that is to say, talking, you know, of this type of bruise, a lesion with extra vascular edema and hemorrhage is not a lesion that I think can occur postmortem."

Dimitriou said, "You don't think it can occur postmortem, but are you still saying that it is impossible?"

Keith responded, "Impossible, yes."

At this time Haddad had a crucial question for Doctor

Keith. "Doctor, in your opinion, the trauma or the injury which resulted in the appearance of the bruises on the face of Patricia Gilmore, in your opinion, did those bruises and trauma occur before death or after death?"

Keith replied, "Oh, before death. I have tried to repeat that as many times as I could."

Chapter
8

The Importance
of Toxicology

Now Doctor Fredrick Rieders was called to testify at Doctor Irvin Gilmore's preliminary hearing on the second day, Thursday, July 30. Rieders, a toxicologist, could provide expert testimony crucial to the Gilmore investigation.

A toxicologist studies the effects of chemicals and biological organisms. Toxicology deals with the chemical makeup of these substances and with finding, identifying, and measuring these chemicals and how they can interact, and how these interactions produce what is harmful to man.

Doctor Rieders began his career working as a junior toxicologist with the chief medical examiner's office of the City of New York, then served on the faculty of Jefferson Medical College in Philadelphia, and eventually became chief toxicologist for the city of Philadelphia. In 1970 he founded National Medical Services, an independent toxicology laboratory.

Doctor Rieders received a request from Reading Hospital physician Doctor John Keith to conduct examinations of the blood samples and tissues of Patricia Gilmore.

Special prosecutor Charles A. Haddad got right to the point. He asked Doctor Rieders, "Can you tell me whether or not you conducted an examination for determination of meperidine in the blood sample submitted to you as being from the body of Patricia Gilmore?"

Rieders stated that he received the specimen on December 2, and the analyses were performed on that day and on the days thereafter for a variety of substances requested including meperidine; the substance meperidine was identified and measured in the specimen, and the result of the analysis was reported on December 8.

Rieders reported that the specimen contained 2.9 micrograms of meperidine per milliliter. Included in the report were comments interpreting the findings.

Haddad asked, "What was that interpretation?"

Rieders answered, "that this finding was consistent with and indicative of acute meperidine poisoning." Rieders said that the concentration was high enough to be life endangering. He stated that a person receiving ordinary, therapeutic doses of around 50 milligrams per single dose, have an average concentration of around 0.05 micrograms per milliliter. The ordinary dosage range is 0.01 to 0.46, although sometimes the high end can be toxic. He stated that the average level in people who die of documented Demerol poisoning is 3.0. The level of 2.9 found in Patricia Gilmore puts this level right on that average.

Doctor Rieders also examined specimens of liver and kidney tissue, and a specimen labeled vomitus. Also examined was subcutaneous fat and skin tissue.

Haddad asked, "Are you stating that your examination of the tissues in A, B, and C led you to believe that each of those injection sites did receive, in fact, the drug meperidine?"

Rieders responded, "Yes, with reasonable certainty."

Haddad asked, "And are you indicating that each of those samples, being A, B, and C, contained a quantity in excess of that contained in the blood?"

Rieders answered, "Yes, grossly in excess ranging all the way from roughly 10 all the way up to close to 400 micrograms in the specimen. So we are speaking of many times greater than in the blood."

It was revealed at this time that a high concentration of meperidine, 13.6 micrograms per gram of liver tissue was present, which is a similar relationship to known fatal cases.

Haddad asked Doctor Rieders what the chemical analysis of Patricia Gilmore's panties reveals.

Rieders replied, "On the exterior, there were, I think it was six—let me refresh my memory—there were six discreet, tiny bloodstains on the panties exteriorly. On the inside of the panties, these same bloodstains were somewhat spread and smeared but still were discreet. Analyses were conducted on these spots, after their blood type had been established, that first of all they were blood and they were human blood and that they were of a certain type. They were extracted and analyzed for meperidine and they were found to contain meperidine and the meperidine was not only identified but measured in those panties. And by virtue of the fact that this had dried down in the blood medium which has cells in it and oxidants, the meperidine was actually changed to what is called meperidinic acid, sort of taking the alcohol of the meperidine but it is a clear-cut meperidine molecule. Meperidine consists of two parts, meperidinic acid and an ethyl alcohol group attached to it and this is dried down, the ethyl alcohol group goes off and what you have left is the meperidinic acid. This is what was identified in the blood spots and measured in the blood spots and that was reported also to you, I believe."

Haddad wanted to know if tests were conducted to see if the drug known as Lomotil would, upon injection, give traces of meperidine.

Rieders testified, "Well, I analyzed the serum for the Lomotil, or for the active ingredient diphenoxylate, which is chemically completely different from meperidine and which is changed in the body in a known manner to something completely different to what meperidine is changed to. The two are easily differentiated, and I have determined that and so have many others, so it's not something that is unique, but it's a well-known fact that these two are two different substances. And I was able to measure the concentration of diphenoxylate, the active ingredient of Lomotil in the serum specimen, and also of meperidine and in the measurement you can—it is obvious the two are separated from each other and are measured separately, and there is no relationship to them. They have two different fingerprints, you might say."

Doctor Rieders indicated that the amount of diphenoxylate in the blood was in the therapeutic range—roughly a hundred times lower than that of the meperidine in the blood specimen.

Haddad asked, "Have you an opinion as to whether the diphenoxylate was a contributing cause of death?"

Rieders said, "I think being a depressant, it may well have speeded up the dying process like any other depressant would. The pathologists say that, under these conditions, the person dies from all the things that were wrong with them but there is one thing without which they would not have died."

Haddad asked, "And what is that?"

Rieders replied, "In this case, in my opinion, the meperidine."

Haddad said, "Are you saying then that meperidine was the agent which caused death to the decedent, Patricia Gilmore?"

Rieders answered, "Yes."

Haddad also questioned Doctor Rieders about his analysis that indicated that the blood serum had a concentration of alcohol in it. Patricia Gilmore had a blood-alcohol concentration of 0.24 percent. He asked about the interaction of the alcohol and meperidine.

Doctor Rieders responded, "Either is at least addictive, so if you have an underlying matrix of an individual who is drunk, and 0.24 is common drunkenness, at least in a chronic drinker they might, you know, maneuver around, I wouldn't trust them to drive certainly or many other things; in an inexperienced person, they may be out cold, so you have this underlying situation of a depressed central nervous system and if you are now superimposing on that an additional depressant of the central nervous system, you will depress it further, not at the same rate—you know, it's sort of a slowing curve, but it certainly will interact unfavorably with the underlying alcohol that is present. Just as I said of the diphenoxylate, they are at least addictive in their presence and actions."

Haddad asked about the matter he examined that was on the glass syringe. "Can you relate to us your findings on this analysis, please?"

Doctor Rieders said his findings were negative for anything identifiable—that it was his understanding that the syringe had previously been tested in another laboratory. Because the syringe and syringe holder had been washed, there were no traces on them that could be identified.

Haddad asked, "Doctor, from your analysis of the samples that you made, are you able to reach any conclusion as to the period of time prior to death that the drug meperidine was administered to the body of Patricia Gilmore?"

Rieders responded that "death occurred more like around an hour after the injection, rather than around a few minutes after the injection, so that it wasn't a kind of an instantaneous situation, but that there was some period of time of perhaps around an hour between the time of the injection and cessation of respiration and death."

Haddad asked, "Doctor, in your experience as a toxicologist, is there any therapeutic purpose for the administration of meperidine in the quantity which resulted in the findings in the body of Patricia Gilmore?"

Doctor Rieders replied, "Not by injection into a person, you know, intramuscular injection into a person, because under 'ordinary circumstances'—I think injection under operating room conditions, to have a continuous infusion of Demerol going in order to offset a certain type of spastic condition for a surgeon to operate on, where there is artificial respiration applied and so forth, but in the sense of the therapeutic administration to a person, under these conditions I know of none, I know of no reason for that dosage."

Dimitriou asked Doctor Rieders if he is familiar with the drug Compazine, which is, like meperidine, a depressant.

Rieders replied, "Well, Compazine is actually a drug that is used against nausea and vomiting. It is a depressant."

Dimitriou asked, "And would that also affect or aggravate the effect of alcohol?"

Rieders said, "The depressant effect if it were present, yes, it is likely to."

Dimitriou continued, "What is the interaction between Lomotil, meperidine, and alcohol where all three are present in the body in the bloodstream?"

Rieders said all of them have a depressant effect on the central nervous system.

Dimitriou asked, "Now, Doctor Rieders, were you asked to determine whether there was any Stadol present?"

Rieders replied, "Specifically, I really don't recall. I was asked to do a general and full determination, which is looking for other substances; in general, any toxically significant levels. I think that Stadol was mentioned. I will have to go back to the original laboratory notebook and see if I was given a list of substances which may have been prescribed to this individual and that may have been among them."

Dimitriou mentioned that there was a second report submitted by Doctor Rieder's laboratory, received just that day. This report was in addition to the one submitted on February 16. He asked Doctor Rieders if this report was more detailed.

Rieders replied, "It has some information in it, some results that were not available at the time of the first report. I really don't know whether or not you want to call it more detailed. It has more additional facts."

Dimitriou asked, "Is there any difference between the blood that is taken from the right heart as opposed to blood taken from the left heart?"

Rieders explained that there would be physiological differences.

Dimitriou pressed, "Would there be any difference in the levels and the readings where it comes from the right heart as opposed to from the left heart?"

Rieders responded, "There can be, yes."

Dimitriou asked, "Isn't it a fact, Doctor Rieders, that where blood is drawn from the right heart, it would possibly show higher levels on the toxicology study—than from in the left heart?"

Doctor Rieders again answered that it may. Rieders stated, when questioned, that blood drawn from the left heart does not give a purer reading, it just gives a different one. He further explained, "Post mortem, you know—if you are speaking of the living patient, there is a difference between blood from a finger and blood drawn from a vein and blood drawn from an artery, even in a living patient. After death, there tends to be an equilibrium between these simply by diffusion because there is no more absorption by the circulation, so if you were to think in terms of preferred, it is preferred for toxicological purposes to obtain blood from the left side of the circulation, as a general rule, to the right side but both of them are commonly obtained and received by the laboratory."

Dimitriou asked, "All right. Now, you indicated on direct examination that, in your opinion, it is highly probable that death occurred about one hour after the injection rather than minutes?"

Rieders said, "Yes. It is my opinion that death, in this case, did not occur within minutes but substantially longer after that; more around an hour or perhaps more and this is for several reasons: Number one, after an intramuscular injection of Demerol, there is a finite period of time that elapses before the peak blood level is reached at which the individual may die; secondly, the distribution of Demerol in this individual, with the high concentrations in the liver and very high concentrations in the urine, indicate that it got from the injection site through the circulation in high concentrations, all the way into the urine, which takes a finite period, and that is why I say more hour rather than minutes."

Dimitriou asked, "Now, add to that if the person who was getting the injection was already under the influence of alcohol at the levels that you found—what is that interaction and what would be the effect on the person who had received an injection, after being at a blood-alcohol level of approximately 0.23 or 0.24?"

Rieders replied that in all likelihood that person would die sooner than that person would have died without the alcohol being present, because the total depressant level would be reached sooner with the added Demerol.

Doctor Rieders also confirmed Dimitriou's scenario that if you have the situation where there is a person with a blood-alcohol level that Patricia Gilmore had, and then gotten more alcohol or an injection of meperidine, the effect on that person, at least the effect on that person after the injection would be the same as one who keeps drinking to the point that they start falling and stumbling and finally pass out.

Rieders added, "That effect would be the same except that the Demerol has a much more serious effect on the respiratory center—so yes, as far as behavioral change is concerned, the Demerol would aggravate, in coordination with alcohol, the whole system. Of course, at the same time, the alcohol would be burning off."

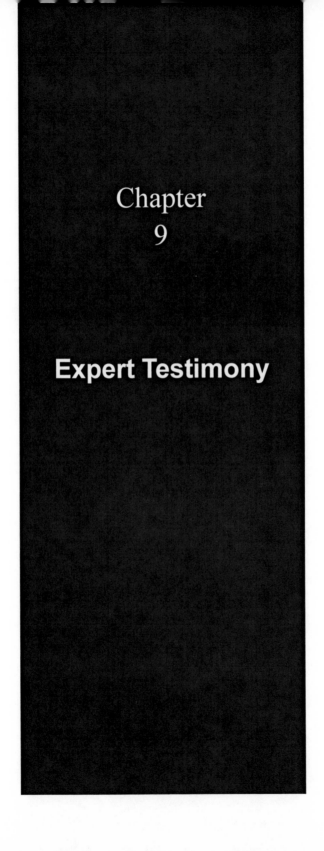

Chapter
9

Expert Testimony

At the end of the second day of the hearing on Thursday, July 30, special prosecutor Charles Haddad requested a continuance until Monday, August 10. District Judge Schultz would be on vacation the week of August 3. Defense attorney Manny Dimitriou had no objections.

People who paid attention to the death of Patricia Gilmore and the subsequent prosecution of Doctor Irvin Gilmore for her murder, should never forget the most important element of the case.

Because of the high amount of the drug Demerol found in her body, the ultimate question is who injected it into her. Demerol killed Patty Gilmore.

Manny Dimitriou's defense strategy had to be to attack the test results. What other defense could there be if the defense conceded that her body was loaded with lethal amounts of the powerful drug?

Dimitriou early on planned to question the handling of the samples procured during the autopsy. His questioning would be thorough; the methods he used to extract even the most trivial information, asking for confirmation over and over, tried the patience of many he grilled. He was looking for "slipups," no matter how insignificant they seemed at the time. He sought to discredit and cast doubt on every aspect of the prosecutor's case.

Where's the documentation? Who touched or handled, or packaged or unpackaged the evidence, removed it, or repackaged it? He also would stir in the crime scene being trampled by the Muhlenberg patrolman who responded to the scene. Had vital evidence been contaminated?

Manny Dimitriou was an excellent defense attorney. That's what he did, and he did it well— very well.

On Monday, August 10, District Judge Schultz reconvened the preliminary hearing for Doctor Irvin Gilmore.

Special prosecutor Haddad called his first witness, Doctor Isadore Mihalakis. Mihalakis had been a practicing forensic pathologist at Sacred Heart Hospital in Allentown, Pennsylvania, since 1969. Mihalakis stated that he had reviewed the autopsy report, reviewed a personal recording Doctor John Keith had made pertinent to the events surrounding the autopsy, and reviewed the toxicology reports with the National Medical Services Laboratory. He also said he reviewed an oral statement of Doctor Gilmore and had spoken with Muhlenberg Police Officers Chief Harley Smith, Detective Barry Hadley, Sergeant Kermit Frantz, and Officer Thomas Dougherty; also Doctor Keith, and Lucy Genslinger of the Muhlenberg Ambulance Service.

Mihalakis also stated he talked by telephone with Doctor Fredrick Rieders and Doctor William Cohn of National Medical Services. He also said he reviewed the autopsy microscopic slides and photographs.

Haddad asked, "Doctor Mihalakis, based on the review of the data and your conversations with the various parties, have you been able to reach a conclusion as to the cause of death of Patricia Gilmore?"

Mihalakis stated that he had, and was asked what his conclusion was.

Mihalakis responded, "Patricia Gilmore died of the combined effects of meperidine and alcohol."

Haddad wanted to know what Mihalakis was basing this professional conclusion on.

Mihalakis said, "The conclusion is based on the levels of the meperidine recovered by the National Medical Services laboratory at Willow Grove, and conversations with Doctor Rieders, and personal experience with the use of this drug and having other—and other cases of toxicological interest. Also, they were based on personal knowledge of alcohol, its effect, distribution and combined effects that it has with drugs."

Haddad wanted to know how the combination of alcohol and meperidine caused the death of Patty Gilmore.

Mihalakis explained, "Okay. She had a 0.24 grams per deciliter alcohol. At that level, alcohol is a depressant of the central nervous system varying from causing sleep, causing a loss of gag reflex—"

Haddad interrupted, "What kind of reflex is that?"

"Gag; if someone were to put something in the mouth, there is some degree of loss of gag reflex, causing loss of visual acuity, auditory acuity, coordination, judgment, and ability to function appropriately given a certain set of circumstances. On the other hand, Demerol is an analgesic, meaning that it takes away pain."

Doctor Mihalakis finished this statement by explaining to Haddad that Demerol is Winthrop Corporation's trade name for meperidine.

He continued to explain, "It is an analgesic meaning by some means it takes away pain and, in the process, causes sedation or meaning that it causes a sleepiness and eventually, in higher amounts, loss of sensitivity or loss of consciousness. It works primarily by in high enough amounts by working on the respiratory center, which is the center of the brain and in so doing it so affects the center so that stimulus or continual breathing is lost. As a result, the body has no longer any desire to breathe. And obviously with loss of breath, death ensues. The combined effects of the meperidine and the alcohol are additive. So that in combination and especially in this particular combination, I feel that they are lethal."

At this time Doctor Mihalakis was shown a series of photographs taken during Patricia Gilmore's autopsy.

Haddad, after confirming that Mihalakis had previously reviewed the photographs and engaged in subsequent discussions, asked him if he would describe the injuries that he observed on the photographs.

Mihalakis stated that the right cheek prominence showed a previously sewn incision or cut area that was removed at the time of the autopsy. At the lower eyelid on the inside portion, there was about a half to three-quarters of an inch fresh bruise. Also, the right side of the nose showed a reddened or mildly bruised area. He said that the left side of the nose—not the bridge, but the side of the nose—showed at least what resembled a braised area and certainly a mildly bruised linear area.

Dimitriou, listening intently to the testimony, interrupted, "What did you say, mildly bruised?"

Doctor Mihalakis responded, "Sort of superficially bruised area."

Haddad followed up by asking Mihalakis if he could make any conclusions as to the cause of the injuries shown in the photographs.

Doctor Mihalakis answered, "The bruises are the hallmarks of a blunt force injury. Singly, they may have been incurred possibly accidentally, walking into something, but that has to be specified. Collectively, if they were all incurred at the same time, I believe it would have to be through the intervention of another party. In other words that they represent a blow or blows rather than an accidental fall. Singly they may represent the fall, but collectively I don't believe they can represent a single fall."

Mihalakis responded to Haddad's additional questioning. "The absence of any bruising or scraping, abrasion of the right eyebrow ridge, and the absence of any bruising or scraping of the bridge of the nose or the tip of the nose. If we are going to depict a fall on a surface, then one has to question as to why the bridge or the tip of the nose show nothing, yet the inner portion, the medial portion of the right lower eyelid shows bruising, and, of course, that is a protected area. The eye is sunken. If that is protected, then why do we not have anything in the areas which protect the—which are the eyebrow ridge, the cheek and the bridge of the nose. Only one of the three shows anything."

Haddad wanted to know if Mihalakis could conclude how the injury was sustained.

Mihalakis replied, "The injury may have been sustained by a blow or blows."

Haddad asked, "Can you further elaborate as to how the blow or blows may have been sustained or rendered?"

Mihalakis followed up, "The most common cause for a black eye is a fist."

Now Haddad displayed a fifth autopsy photograph, and asked the doctor to comment.

Mihalakis said, "Okay, No. 5 is an overview showing the skull after it has been—after the skull has been incised and after the incision of the skull itself through the saw; at the time in the morgue it had been made. It shows the left forehead area. It shows a freshly bruised area, I forget the exact dimension—I will have it for you in a minute. It is a fresh bruise which was measured by Doctor Keith as 1.5 centimeters in diameter. That would put us into the area of about nine-sixteenths of an inch."

Haddad now referred to what the photograph of the rear skull area shows.

Mihalakis said, "In the back of the head, it shows a circular fresh bruise of the scalp and, based on Doctor Keith's dictation, it is 15 millimeters in diameter, again in the region of nine-sixteenths of an inch."

Haddad asked, "And finally, will you look at the photograph of the hand, please, and describe to us any bruise or injury you see thereon? Is there any injury shown on that—"

Mihalakis said, "Yes. At the—adjacent to the knuckle at the base of the left index finger there is what appears to be a freshly bruised area on—about an inch in greatest dimension."

Dimitriou asked Mihalakis about his statement that the injuries pictured are the hallmark of blunt force injury and that he also indicated they could have been caused by someone walking into something, if each one is taken singly.

He asked, "Collectively, your opinion would be that they would have been caused by blows, correct?"

Mihalakis stated that was correct.

Dimitriou continued, "Now the fact is, Doctor, that this is at best speculation or a guess on your part, isn't it?"

Mihalakis replied with a question, "No. What made you think that?"

Dimitriou was now showing why he had a reputation for being the epitome of craftiness in casting a blanket of doubt upon a prosecution witness. Obviously if the injuries occurred singly, at different times—that would indicate they resulted from falls made at different times.

He admonished the doctor, "Just answer my question. Is there anything that you have reviewed that could make you state, with a reasonable degree of medical certainty, that these bruises were not caused singly."

Mihalakis replied, "Oh, surely."

He asked, "—am I correct?"

Mihalakis answered, "No. I have reviewed something which would lead one to believe they may not have been caused singly."

Dimitriou kept up the pressure: "What have you reviewed that is causing you to say that they have not been caused singly?"

Mihalakis shot back, "I didn't say that they haven't, they may not have been."

Dimitriou responded, "They may not have been?"

Mihalakis said, "The fact that they are all the same age."

Dimitriou persisted, "They are all the same age. By the same token, Doctor, they may have been caused singly, isn't that right, on multiple occasions, all at the same time?"

Mihalakis, responding to Dimitriou's suggestion that they may have been caused singly, stated that they could have been caused within a very short period of time, and responded positively to Dimitriou's suggestion that it's possible, provided the appropriate implement or at least the appropriate object that was struck was found.

Dimitriou asked, "Is that necessary? Is it necessary that you find the object to make that determination, that they were caused singly?"

Mihalakis responded, "Well, you can't get it from nothing."

Dimitriou asked, "Well, suppose, Doctor, someone stumbles and falls and strikes a sofa or strikes a leather-padded board. Now that is a blunt object, is it not?"

Mihalakis agreed, and responded to Dimitriou's suggestion that a fall on that kind of object could cause this kind of a bruise: "Well, you see again you are specifically saying something is padded. Something that is padded gives. If something gives, why do we have such a well-localized linear bruised area on the right side of the flaring of the nose? I have no objection, but I mean, all I ask is—you gave me a specific situation in which this occurred, and I would have simply agreed with you."

Dimitriou continued to go over and over the details of what Mihalakis had previously stated, looking for conflicting testimony. He asked the doctor if his opinion was these bruises could have been caused by walking or falling if they had been caused singly, or the bruises were caused by blows if they were caused collectively.

Mihalakis answered, "No. You see, you have got to read it back. I said provided we have the proper setting in which they were received."

Dimitriou didn't need to remind the doctor that he wasn't at the setting, and neither was he. "So that neither one of us being at the setting, it is a fact that these blows may have been caused by a fall or walking into an object, just as they may have been caused by a blow, isn't that a fair statement?"

Mihalakis didn't agree, and explained why. "They could not have been caused by walking into an object. One would have to walk into multiple objects, you know, would have to run into the right side of the nose, the left side of the nose, then, you know, the forehead, then the right lower lid, then the cheek."

Dimitriou asked the doctor if he agreed that walking into different objects over a span of approximately one hour would result in the same kind of bruising. Mihalakis stated that he would have to agree under that type of hypothetical situation.

Dimitriou wanted to know what the doctor had to say about the bruise on the back of the head.

Mihalakis said, "That is an exposed, prominent area.

Either a fall, either walking backward into something or a blow; you know, it's an exposed, prominent area, either mechanism could work."

Dimitriou came back, "So that with regard to the bruise in the back of the head and the bruise over the left forehead, they could have been caused by a fall or walking into objects, just as easily or equally as by a blow?" Mihalakis agreed.

Dimitriou continued with his grueling questioning. "Doctor, could a blow on the nose have caused the bruises on both sides of the nose?" Mihalakis agreed.

"And if a blow on the nose could cause the bruise on both sides of the nose, then a fall, in which the person falls on their nose, would have the same effect?"

Mihalakis responded, "No, sir."

Dimitriou responded, "It would not?"

Mihalakis explained, "No, sir. No, because you have to strike it."

Dimitriou asked, "The what?"

Mihalakis said, "The tip of the nose first."

Dimitriou continued, "So if someone falls and strikes the tip of their nose, wouldn't it have the same effect, as far as bruising, as one who was struck on the tip of the nose with a blow?"

Mihalakis responded, "We are talking about the injuries to the side?"

Dimitriou stated that he was talking about the injuries to the side of the nose shown in the autopsy photographs.

Mihalakis stated, "Well, why don't we have anything on the tip? I mean, if you are falling—"

Dimitriou snapped back, "I am not the doctor. I am asking you if a blow on the front part of the tip of the nose, as well as a fall on the tip of the nose, would not cause bruising on the side of the nose?"

Mihalakis confirmed, "That's correct, sir; it would not."

Dimitriou now wanted to know how a person's physical behavior would be affected when someone is under the influence of alcohol, then comes under the influence of meperidine.

Mihalakis said that judgment would be impaired, and the person would be likely to make wrong choices. Alertness would be affected, the individual would be sleepy and tired, also coordination would be impaired, staggering to some degree. The doctor explained that an individual's sensitivity varies. Vision, hearing, and the gag reflex would be suppressed, and the attention span would be considerably impaired.

Dimitriou asked, "Tell me doctor, 0.24, do you consider that a high level of blood alcohol in the blood system of an individual?"

Mihalakis replied, "Yes, sir; I do."

Dimitriou followed up, "Now, it is not uncommon for a person with a blood alcohol of 0.24 in their blood system to be stumbling and falling and having difficulty keeping their balance, is it?"

Mihalakis said, "That's correct."

Dimitriou wanted the doctor to confirm that stumbling and falling is consistent with an individual who has a 0.24 level of blood alcohol. The doctor said that he didn't know what the lawyer meant by consistent, but confirmed that it is possible for someone with that amount of alcohol in the blood to stumble and fall, having difficulty keeping balance.

Dimitriou asked, "Let's go a step farther: isn't it probable?"

Mihalakis said, "Not necessarily. It all depends on what the obstruction is. Now, I have seen someone with 0.24 take their dog for a walk. The only problem is, if they stumble and fall, they have a great difficulty getting up. So I think we have to answer these questions in light of a certain setting. Do you see what I am trying to obtain for you?"

Dimitriou asked, "Now, if we add to that the additive of the meperidine, what is the effect on their behavior, physical behavior?"

Mihalakis replied, "Marked depression."

Dimitriou asked, "In other words, in the earlier stages, the probability of stumbling and falling against objects or walking into things would be considerably enhanced; wouldn't it?"

Mihalakis responded, "Well, yes. We are assuming that we have not reached a point of say unconsciousness,"

Before Dimitriou continued on his line of questioning, he asked about one statement the doctor had made that the most common cause of a black eye is a fist. He wanted to know some other causes.

Mihalakis answered, "Doorknobs." He continued, "Elbows. I suppose falling asleep on a drink could also do it. I mean, you know—something circular which is capable of getting into the orbit without causing injury to the tissue around the orbit."

Dimitriou asked, "So by stating that a black eye is most commonly caused by a fist, you by no means are excluding other common causes; correct?"

Mihalakis said, "That's correct, sir."

Dimitriou now wanted to know about the therapeutic dosage of meperidine. Doctor Mihalakis replied that that varies widely. Dimitriou wanted to know the ranges.

The doctor responded, "It goes anywhere from about a .2 to about .6, even .7 micrograms per milliliter."

At this time Doctor Mihalakis explained that an injection

of 50 to 75 milligrams of meperidine will reach a peak concentration in the blood level of anywhere from .2 to .6 or .7.

Dimitriou asked, "And that would depend on the individual, correct?"

Mihalakis responded, "The individual, the absorption—multiple various sundry factors."

Later in the questioning attorney Dimitriou turned his attention to the needle marks on Patricia Gilmore's buttock.

He inquired, "I am asking you—first of all, do you know how many needle marks there were?"

Mihalakis answered, "Anywhere from between two to about four." He later added that there could conceivably be up to six.

Dimitriou asked Mihalakis if he had reviewed the photographs, then asked if he can find six needle marks on the right buttock.

The doctor replied, "I can find five without any problem."

Dimitriou shot back, "I didn't ask you five. Try to answer my questions. You just said anywhere up to six. Now, you show me where there are six."

Mihalakis referred to the photographs and pointed out individually five needle marks, and then indicating a possible sixth one.

Dimitriou asked, "Which possibly?"

The doctor, still pointing to the autopsy photograph, replied, "That conceivably—I don't think anybody can tell [*indicating*]. And this is an if [*indicating*]."

Dimitriou stated, "If we eliminate the ifs. Nowhere in Doctor Keith's report did he find six needle marks."

Mihalakis responded, "No, but you said have I reviewed the other material and I think somewhere along the line somebody said something about up to six."

Dimitriou now asked the question he was laying the groundwork to ask. He asked, "Doctor, based on the review of that data, the autopsy report, the photograph, et cetera, et cetera, can you give an opinion as to how long before death any of those needle marks were made?"

Mihalakis replied, "Okay. Based on the whole thing, in probably less than six hours."

Dimitriou responded, "So based on all the information—so that we are clear—that you have made available to you, autopsy report, personal recording of the autopsy by Doctor Keith, toxicology reports, police offense reports, oral statement of Doctor Gilmore, photographs and slides and microscopic slides, personal conversations with Doctor Rieders, Doctor Cohn, and Doctor Keith, Chief Smith, officers Hadley, Frantz and Dougherty, and Mr. Haddad, in your opinion, these needle marks were made up to six hours prior to the time of death, is that correct?"

Mihalakis said, "That's correct."

Dimitriou asked, "Now, will you tell us what you base that opinion on?"

The doctor said that Doctor Keith described them as "fresh," and after Dimitriou challenged him as to what his definition of "fresh" was, he responded, "Less than six hours."

Dimitriou and Mihalakis started an exchange that began with Dimitriou asking if the definition is acceptable in medical journals, and is the term defined anywhere as anything less than six hours. Mihalakis explained that the word "fresh" refers to the time lapse beyond which tissue changes. He explained that some authorities say you have to stretch that up to twelve hours; that is the very maximum.

Dimitriou asked, "And if some authorities define fresh up to twelve hours, then these needle marks could have been made in excess of six hours; isn't that right?"

Mihalakis replied, "No, because you said based on my review of all the material, okay."

Dimitriou asked, "Now, tell me what else, in addition to Doctor Keith."

Mihalakis responded, "Well, you know, we have Demerol metabolites which do not indicate a time that long. We have Demerol metabolites that indicated up to three hours."

Mihalakis explained that for him to determine a time of death he could only go by what Doctor Rieders said, how long it would take to build to those hours. He said that Doctor Keith did the autopsy, but he didn't do any drug levels. The doctor said that from his visual examination of the tissues, you can conceivably go up to twelve hours, more likely less than six hours. He reminded Dimitriou that he had given him the freedom to take all the parameters into account—"the fact they have no Demerol metabolites to speak of, you know, indicates that she died very soon thereafter. Otherwise, you would have more metabolites."

Dimitriou asked, "What are metabolites?"

Mihalakis answered, "A product of the metabolism of Demerol, of meperidine."

Dimitriou asked, "And how soon after injection do they start to show in the tissue to become evident?"

Mihalakis explained that it takes several hours, toxicologically, up to three. Asked if it could have been more than three hours or three hours is not a firm stance, he replied, "Again, you would have to go to the toxicologist, go back to the metabolites of Demerol, but he doesn't have enough to indicate any significance of metabolism. In only one place do we talk about meperidinic acid.

Later Dimitriou asked, "Doctor, do you know the trajectory of these needle marks?"

Mihalakis replied, "Yes. It's supposed to be somewhat in a cephalad—which is toward the head.

Dimitriou asked the doctor to confirm that people who use drugs commonly inject themselves in the buttocks.

Mihalakis asked, "First of all, what sort of injection are you talking about?"

Dimitriou followed up, "Any injection. I'm talking about an injection with a syringe and a needle. Is there anything uncommon about a person to inject themselves in the buttocks?"

Mihalakis said there was.

Haddad objected to Dimitriou's questioning Doctor Mihalakis, that he found no cases, in his seventeen years of pathology, where persons have injected themselves in the buttocks. Judge Schultz sustained the objection. Haddad pointed out that wasn't the doctor's testimony. The question is, is it uncommon?

Next Dimitriou asked, "Have you found cases where persons have injected themselves in the buttocks, in your experience?"

Mihalakis explained, "As part of an overall multiple injection picture, yes, but as isolated buttocks only, no."

Dimitriou then concluded that the doctor had seen people who injected themselves in other places as well as in the buttocks.

Mihalakis replied, "Actually, the sides of the hips, not the back; the sides of the hips. I have never run across anybody injecting themselves that far back."

Haddad now objected to Dimitriou asking the doctor what the trajectory of the needle is when someone injects themselves in the buttocks. Haddad's objection was that because the doctor never saw anybody inject themselves in the buttocks he was not able to answer that question.

Dimitriou quickly asked the doctor, "Can you answer that question?"

Mihalakis explained, "A lot depends on how you hold the needle, you know, but it's not the easiest way to use the injection finger if you are going in an upwards direction. Generally speaking, one holds the syringe and pushes with the thumb. It's kind of awkward to point a needle towards the head."

Dimitriou said that is what he wants to find out. He wanted to know how much does a two cc syringe hold in fluid, and what is the trajectory when a person makes an injection, or when an injection is made by someone who is trained such as a nurse or a doctor; and what is the trajectory of the needle according to standard form.

Mihalakis said, "Generally, it's either upward, downward. I don't think it has any specific direction or, you know, backward meaning toward the midline."

Dimitriou responded, "It's whether upward, downward— or toward the midline. And that is the way a doctor or a nurse would normally make an injection in the buttocks area; is that your testimony?" The doctor confirmed that it was.

Dimitriou wanted to know if he ever heard of bread-slicing the buttocks during an autopsy to determine if a person has old needle marks.

Mihalakis replied, "Again, you have got to go by what kind of needle marks or what kind of medication are we talking about. Certainly with meperidine, okay, the material is an irritant. It's been known to cause sterile abscesses. It's caused inflammatory responses, you know, they lead to hardening of the fat, they lead to scarring of the muscle, you know, and that in turn causes discoloration of the overlying skin. You can feel these things, if somebody would be an addict for quite a while."

Dimitriou responded, "But if you don't know whether the person has been an addict and you are doing an autopsy and you find needle marks, wouldn't it be good practice to bread-slice the buttocks to find if there are any old needle marks?"

Mihalakis replied, "Well, I would bread-slice the entire body, while we are at it."

Dimitriou said, "We are just talking about the buttocks."

Mihalakis said, "I don't—it is not the commonest location to give yourself needle marks. One of the hallmarks of an addict, he uses accessible sites. You know, it's not really terribly accessible, the back of the buttocks."

Dimitriou said it's not impossible either, and then, as if he met a dead-end brick wall, abruptly switched back to issues dealing with the bruises. He wanted to know how the doctor described the bruises: being severe, mild, light, or slight based on his observations and what he had reviewed.

Mihalakis said, "They were of sufficient severity to cause blood to leak out of the vessels, to damage the tissues so that the vessel was sufficiently destroyed to cause leakage of blood into the surrounding tissues."

Dimitriou asked, "Now, I am still back to my question. Do you consider these severe bruises, mild bruises or slight bruises?"

Mihalakis replied, "As opposed to what? They were enough to cause tissue damage. They were enough to cause edema."

Dimitriou and Mihalakis sparred back and forth about the severity of blows, and the resulting classification of bruises.

Finally Dimitriou asked, "Well, tell me something, Doctor, if there is a bruise before death, which has been caused before death, wouldn't that be substantially aggravated if the person was in a face-down position?"

The doctor explained that the bruises are aggravated because some of the blood settles and seeps out of the damaged vessels and goes into the bruise. The bruise will be aggravated somewhat, but not of any great consequence.

Dimitriou, trying to draw conclusions favorable to the defendant, dwelled on the aggravation issue. "But what you are saying is, that a bruise would be somewhat aggravated, a bruise that was caused before death, would be somewhat aggravated by a face-down position, correct?"

Mihalakis stuck by his contention. "That is true, leaving a wide spectrum of openings but primarily minimal. You would have a marked amount if there would be some decomposition. We have no decomposition here."

Dimitriou now asked, "By the way, are you familiar with the drug called Lomotil?"

Mihalakis said it stops diarrhea, that it contains diphenoxylate and has an opiate base.

Dimitriou asked, "Is it similar to Demerol?"

Mihalakis said it is not, despite also having an opiate base. It doesn't have any sedative properties, and it doesn't have any properties to stop respiration, unless taken in massive overdoses.

Dimitriou asked, "What is the effect, Doctor, of a combination of Lomotil and Demerol?"

Mihalakis replied, "So long as we are talking about therapeutic quantities of Lomotil, it's inconsequential."

Dimitriou responded, "It's inconsequential. And what if you add alcohol to it? So now you have alcohol, Demerol and a therapeutic level of Lomotil, is Lomotil an additive to the other two?"

Mihalakis stated, "If it's in the therapeutic range, I don't believe it, no."

Dimitriou continued, "So that I understand your testimony correctly, Doctor, you are saying that it took approximately

600 milligrams of Demerol injected to reach the 2.9 micrograms per milliliter in this case; is that what your are saying?"

Mihalakis answered, "That is my testimony based on the toxicology report. Actually, to be exact, he said greater than 600 milligrams, Mr. Dimitriou."

Dimitriou confirmed it was the doctor's belief that the alcohol in Patty Gilmore's body, with a reading of 0.24, was the result of her self-consumption of alcoholic beverages. He also confirmed that based on all the information made available the time of death was unknown.

Mihalakis said, "Well, we know it occurred somewhere around three hours after the injections, okay."

Dimitriou said, "But we don't know what time the injections were, do we?"

Mihalakis stated that it's known that she went to bed around 2:30, and that she was found at 8:00, and that doesn't leave too many hours' leeway, and the alcohol was consumed sometime prior to that time span.

Dimitriou asked, "So that I am correct that the 0.24 blood alcohol could have been considerably higher several hours before that?" He continued, "Now, all I am asking you very simply, is that if the blood level or the blood alcohol in her body at the time of the autopsy was 0.24, is it possible that her blood-alcohol level prior to death, an hour, or two hours, or three hours prior to death could have been considerably higher; isn't that right?"

Mihalakis stated he didn't know what considerably means—he mentioned that the rate of metabolism, say 20 milliliters per hour, and the assumption that the last alcoholic beverage was drunk at 2 a.m. could create a situation that would allow us to develop some reasonable, concrete examples.

Chapter
10

More Witnesses

During the afternoon of Wednesday, July 29, 1981, Muhlenberg Police Officer Thomas Dougherty, a 3-year veteran of that force, ambulance attendant Lucille Genslinger and Gilmore family friend, and Trooper Barrie Pease testified at the preliminary hearing.

Dougherty's often-repeated account of what happened that Thanksgiving morning would be reexamined, and now retold under oath in a formal court setting. He was the first to be called by Special Prosecutor Haddad, and confirmed that he was on duty on November 27, 1980, and went to the Gilmore residence at 4100 Kutztown Road, Temple, Pennsylvania, after overhearing an ambulance dispatch over the emergency radio system.

Dougherty stated that he was only a block and a half away from the house when he heard the dispatch, and as a result went to the residence to see if he could offer any assistance.

"When I arrived at the location, I pulled in front of the house. I was northbound on Kutztown Road at the time. I was met at the curb by a young man. He told me that he believes Pat was dead, to hurry up."

Dougherty explained that because he knew Doctor Gilmore, and had been given his employment physical examination and other treatment by the doctor, he immediately recognized the house as Gilmore's.

Officer Dougherty said that after arriving at the scene he went upstairs to the second-floor bedroom where Doctor Gilmore and Patricia were lying on the bed. He felt the body to see if he could find a pulse, which he could not. At this time the Muhlenberg Ambulance arrived.

"I got Doctor Gilmore to go downstairs to the kitchen with me." He said the reason he did that was because he didn't want

Doctor Gilmore there when the ambulance personnel were removing the body.

Haddad wanted to know if Dougherty talked to the doctor while in the kitchen, and if he did, what did they talk about.

Dougherty said, "I asked him when was the last time he saw his wife alive. He said the night before; he had gone to bed early. His wife and his daughter-in-law were sitting in the kitchen. I had asked him if his wife was on any kind of medication. His response was none that he knows of. I asked Doctor Gilmore if his wife was depressed over anything. He said that he didn't think so."

Haddad wanted to know if Dougherty conducted any kind of preliminary search of the house and particularly the room where Patricia Gilmore was located.

Dougherty replied that he did and didn't observe anything out of the ordinary in the room.

He said, "I received information from Doctor Gilmore's son relative to a missing item from the doctor's bag, which was supposed to be a syringe. I searched the upstairs rooms and found the syringe in the back room of the house that is a dressing-room-type room."

Dougherty said the room is across the hall from the Gilmores' bedroom. He found the syringe on a table across from a dressing chair, a lounge-type chair.

Haddad asked, "You say you found a syringe; was there a needle in the syringe?"

Dougherty said there wasn't a needle in the syringe; there was a small amount of a brownish-type liquid in the syringe, but no needle. He testified that he searched all over the upstairs for a needle, but didn't find one.

Officer Dougherty said he made no further examination of

the syringe, didn't try to identify the contents of it, and then transported it to the Pennsylvania State Police Laboratory in Bethlehem, Pennsylvania.

Haddad asked Dougherty if he knew Patty Gilmore, and for how long. And asked him to identify a photograph of her, which he did. Dougherty replied he knew Patty Gilmore by name, for about three years.

Dougherty explained that he had never been in the upstairs of the Gilmore home before, so he wouldn't have known if there was anything unusual that would have attracted his attention. He repeated that Doctor Gilmore was agitated, crying and pacing around as if he were in shock—he seemed dazed.

Dimitriou asked, "Now, Officer Dougherty, the young man that you referred to who told you that he believed Pat was dead, you should hurry up; can you identify him?" Dougherty said it was Doctor Gilmore's son, Barry. He said he asked him who he was and he told him.

Dimitriou asked Dougherty what he felt was a crucial question: "When you went to the bedroom, what position was Patricia Gilmore in on the bed?"

Dougherty replied, "She was on her back." Dougherty also stated that Patty's skin was very cold and it had a grayish tint to it. He said he didn't know if her body was stiff because all he felt was her neck to see if he could feel her pulse.

Dimitriou asked, "Now, Officer Dougherty, did you observe anything unusual other than the fact that she was cold and that there was a grayish tint to her complexion? Did you notice anything unusual about her face or anything else, make any observations?"

Dougherty said he didn't notice anything. When asked if he

saw any bruises, marks, or cuts, he responded, "The room was poorly lit. I did not see anything other than the grayish color."

Dougherty also testified that he did not see any bruises or contusions on her face at the hospital, however he noticed several needle marks on her right upper thigh, pointed out to him by the emergency room doctor, Doctor George Kershner.

Later during redirect examination, Charles Haddad asked Dougherty, "Officer Dougherty, even though your report indicates that you observed one injection mark on the body of Patricia Gilmore, can you tell us what, in fact, you did observe that day?"

Dougherty replied, "I observed several. They were not counted. I can't recall, you know, by looking at them how many there were."

Dimitriou asked again about the syringe, in particular the results of the laboratory tests.

"Did you get a report on it?" Dougherty said that a Muhlenberg detective had the report, and even though he personally transported it to the state police laboratory, he didn't recall if the report was mailed to him.

Dimitriou asked, "Do you know if anybody found a needle?" Dougherty said nobody did, and that he looked for the needle.

Dimitriou asked him what time he got to the Gilmore house. Dougherty said he got there at approximately 9:02 a.m., and left about twenty or twenty-five minutes later—it seems like it was a relatively small amount of time to be on the scene. At this point Dougherty should have called his superiors and requested assistance from police officers experienced in investigating suspicious deaths. He didn't know what caused Patty Gilmore's death, common sense would tell a police officer that when a young woman is found dead in her bed, and the cause of death is not obvious, it should be treated as possibly suspicious. The premises should be considered a possible crime scene. The old adage, rather safe than sorry, definitely applied here.

Dimitriou asked, "The medical bag; where did you find that?"

Dougherty responded, "The medical bag was in a front room—I call it a study type room. It was adjacent to Doctor Gilmore's and his wife's bedroom and across the hall from what I considered a dressing room. It's at the top of the stairs to the left."

Dimitriou asked, "Did you make any determination as to whether the bag was found initially by anyone else? In other words, from Barry Gilmore or from Doctor Gilmore, did they tell you where they found the bag in the morning?"

Dougherty replied, "No. Barry Gilmore showed me where the bag was when I first saw it."

Dimitriou asked, "When you first saw it?"

Dougherty replied, "That's correct." Dougherty said there was no question as to whether the bag was there when he found it.

When asked he did say he talked to daughter-in-law Linda Gilmore while at the hospital. Linda told him she and Patty were in the kitchen until about 2 a.m., when Linda went to bed.

Dimitriou asked, "Now, did you make any inspection of the medical bag to determine its contents or inspect any of the contents in the bag?"

Dougherty answered, "I looked in the medical bag. A chrome instrument, syringe protector or—I don't know what they are called—was there, an empty one. There were vials of medication; I don't know what else. An inventory was not taken, okay?"

Dimitriou asked him what time he went to the hospital. Dougherty replied, "Directly."

Dimitriou wanted to know if Dougherty observed anything unusual, and what was Doctor Gilmore's condition.

Dougherty said he talked to Doctor Kershner about an autopsy, and requested that the Muhlenberg Police be contacted when the autopsy was scheduled so that somebody from their office would be present.

Dimitriou questioned, "But who raised the question of an autopsy?"

Dougherty said that he did. "I told Doctor Kershner that when he got in touch with somebody from the coroner's office that I requested an autopsy be done."

Haddad called on Lucille Genslinger, the attendant with the Muhlenberg Ambulance that Responded to the Gilmore house on November 27.

Genslinger testified that upon arrival at the house, Barry Gilmore met them outside on the lawn and from there took them to the second-floor bedroom. She stated that she found Patricia Gilmore on the bed—the body was cold, was blue, and rigor mortis was starting to set in. Genslinger said she did not conduct any assistance to the body, but she did check for a pulse.

Haddad asked, "Why did you not offer any assistance?"

Genslinger said, "Due to the condition of the body and also with Doc present, I felt if she could have been resuscitated, he probably would have tried before our arrival."

She said that crewmembers did not administer any kind of injections to the body, and then they transferred it over to what is called a bone litter—a flexible, heavy-canvas-type litter used for going downstairs. The body was taken downstairs and, still on the bone litter, placed on the ambulance litter.

Haddad asked, "How was the body clothed?"

Genslinger replied, "A nightshirt and underwear."

Genslinger said that the body was secured in the ambulance. She explained that the bone litter has three straps that secure the body, and a bar that runs alongside the ambulance and locked in secures an additional three straps on the ambulance litter, and in the ambulance itself, the litter. She stated that she rode in the back of the ambulance while the body was transported to the hospital.

Haddad had an important question to ask. "At any time from the time you entered the home until the time the body was taken to the hospital in the vehicle, did you at any time observe that the body was bumped or bruised in any way?"

Genslinger said, "No." She also said that she didn't see anything hit the body, and that it was secured in the vehicle in a way that it did not bump or touch the sides of the vehicle.

Haddad followed up, "Did you see anything come in contact with the body at all?"

Genslinger replied, "Nothing." She said that when the ambulance arrived at the hospital the body was taken, still on the ambulance litter, to Room F, and from there it was transferred from the ambulance litter to the hospital litter.

Haddad wanted to know if she noticed the body strike any object or any object strike the body during this movement. Genslinger stated that she did not.

Dimitriou, during his cross-examination of Genslinger, went over some details of the ambulance operations with her, and then posed a crucial question, "What was the position of the body?"

Genslinger replied, "She was laying on her back."

Dimitriou asked, "And where did you take her pulse?"

Genslinger said she took her pulse at the carotid artery in her neck, at which time she had the opportunity to observe her face.

Dimitriou asked, "Did you observe any bruises or contusions on her face?" Genslinger said she did not.

He followed up, stating that the trip to the hospital in the ambulance took place after 9:00 in the morning, and that there was daylight and it was clear outside, and confirmed with Genslinger that the face was not covered while the body was in the ambulance.

"So you had additional time to observe the face while it was in the ambulance; is that right?"

She responded, "Yes."

Dimitriou asked, "Did you observe any bruises or contusions at any time on the face?"

Genslinger replied that she did not.

Now Haddad called on long-time Gilmore friend Trooper Barrie Pease to testify. Haddad was interested in all the details previously recounted in detail by Pease about his meetings and conversations with Gilmore during the days and weeks following Patty's death.

Pease recalled, "Doc told me that he had been in the district attorney's office, and that they had been questioning about Patty's death, and that somebody in the district attorney's office or the DA's office thought he had killed Patty.

"He told me that Patty had died from an overdose of Demerol; that she had high blood alcohol content; that the night before she died, she had been sick and had been vomiting and he had given her some injection of vitamin B-12, I think he said, and meperidine to take care of the vomiting and the sickness from the alcohol."

Haddad asked, "When was the next time you had a conversation with Doctor Gilmore?"

Pease said that Gilmore called him on the twenty-second of December, a day before Pease was to leave the state for the holidays, and told him that his son Barry was up from Florida and that he would like to give the gun Pease was holding for him to Barry. Pease said he took the gun back to Gilmore's house, where he explained to Barry how to take the gun to a gun dealer and transfer the registration into his name. Pease said that after he handed the gun to Barry, Gilmore asked if he could talk to him upstairs.

"Doc took me up in the hallway at the top of the steps and showed me the bedroom that he had shared with Patty, which was on the left-hand side of the hallway as you go in. He told me that the night that the—or the morning rather—that the police had come, when he woke up that morning, Patty had been laying diagonally across the bed next to him. Laying next to her was a stethoscope; that on the headboard of the bed was a cotton ball with some bloodstains on it, and that there was a syringe with a bent needle in a grayish-colored ashtray on the night stand next to the bed."

Haddad questioned him, "Did he say what, if anything, he did with these items?"

Pease said, "He told me he threw the syringe away; that he threw the cotton ball away; that he moved the ashtray from the nightstand to a small table that was in the hall outside of the bed- room, and that he put the stethoscope back into his medical bag and then I'm not clear on whether he said he moved the medical bag from a room into Patty's room or from Patty's room into another room."

Pease said that Gilmore told him that he had not told the

district attorney's office about the stethoscope or the cotton ball or about moving the ashtray. During that conversation Gilmore told Pease that another attorney had referred him to Manny Dimitriou. Pease stated that he told Gilmore to go see Dimitriou and tell him the same story.

Haddad asked, "You indicated, Trooper Pease, that the second conversation, after the death of Patricia Gilmore, that you had with Doctor Gilmore took place at the Whit-Mar Inn, and, at that time, he indicated to you that he had administered vitamins and meperidine to Patricia Gilmore?"

Pease stated, "That's correct."

Haddad followed up, "During any of the time that you have worked as a state police trooper, have you ever come in contact with the drug or substance meperidine?"

Pease said that he couldn't recall ever having any contact with the drug, and that he didn't remember ever hearing the name of the drug before.

Haddad asked, "Prior to hearing the name of the drug meperidine from Doctor Gilmore, had any of the police from Muhlenberg mentioned that name to you?"

Pease's reply was, "No, sir."

Dimitriou wanted to know how often he had seen Gilmore and Patty at the Whit-Mar Inn. Pease said from the year that he knew Patty, he thought about once a week, sometimes less, sometimes twice a week. Pease explained that he only got to know Gilmore socially about the time he got to know Patty. Before that, it was a professional association.

Dimitriou wanted to know if Gilmore and Patty would always leave together.

"I believe so. I would say as a general rule they did. I can't remember any specific instance when Doc and Patty left separately."

Dimitriou asked, "When you saw Doctor Gilmore at the Whit-Mar Inn about a week after the death, you told him you were sorry about Patty dying; correct? How would you describe his condition at that time?"

Pease said, "He was emotionally upset."

"Was he drinking?"

Pease said he didn't recall if Gilmore was drinking.

Dimitriou grilled Pease about whether Gilmore and Patty drank an excessive amount of alcohol, and if Gilmore ever left to go home while Patty stayed.

Pease didn't think it was a fair statement that on the occasions he had seen them at the inn that they were consuming considerable amounts of alcohol.

Dimitriou asked, "You don't think so?"

"No. The owner of the Whit-Mar Inn, Harry Kore, as a matter of fact had a policy that Doc had two drinks while he was at the Whit-Mar and after that—"

Dimitriou asked, "Do you know what he drank?"

Pease said he thought Gilmore drank martinis. He said that he wasn't aware that the inn had any limit on the amount Patty could drink. He stated that he saw Patty drink more than two drinks while he was in her and Gilmore's company.

Pease said that the second time he saw Gilmore at the Whit-Mar after Patty's death was on December 14 or 15, in the evening. He said that Gilmore was alone and had been drinking; he said he observed him drink maybe two drinks during the two hours he was there.

Dimitriou asked Pease if the conversation with Gilmore took place at the Whit-Mar when Gilmore disclosed that he was at the district attorney's office.

Pease said that it was, and said, "As I remember, that conversation took place at the bar. Doc and I were seated at the end of the bar and owner of the Whit-Mar, Harry Kore, was there for part of it. He was working tending bar, so that he was there for part of it and gone for part of it."

Pease explained that Kore at times would walk over and stand right next to Gilmore at the end of the bar.

Dimitriou said, "He was standing right next to Doc, so you would assume that he was able to hear what Doc was telling you?"

Pease answered yes, and confirmed that Gilmore had told him that Patty had died from an overdose of Demerol and a high blood-alcohol content.

Dimitriou asked if Gilmore indicated where he got that information. Pease answered he did not.

Dimitriou asked, "Do you recall specifically what he said to you?

Pease answered, "His exact words?"

Dimitriou said, "Yes."

Pease said he didn't recall his exact words, and of course Dimitriou spoke up, "So what you are telling us is a summary?"

Pease said it wasn't, that he was paraphrasing the conversation.

Dimitriou said, "Paraphrase of the conversation, as you recall it?"

Pease said, "That's correct."

Pease stated that after the holidays, during the first or second week of January, he contacted Chief Smith of the Muhlenberg Police.

Then Dimitriou jumped to the night before Patty died. He asked Pease if Gilmore had related to him anything that transpired the night before Patty's death.

Pease said that Gilmore didn't confide in him about whether

they had been at a party, but he did say that Patty had told him a couple of weeks before that Gilmore's son and daughter-in-law would be up from Florida visiting. Patty was planning to cook Thanksgiving dinner for a group of people.

Dimitriou asked, "You indicated that Doctor Gilmore told you that Patty Gilmore was sick the night before?" Pease acknowledged that Gilmore told him that the night before she died she was throwing up and had diarrhea.

Pease said, "My assumption was that Patty had been drinking the night before and, due to the drinking and the high blood alcohol, she had been sick that night and was throwing up and had diarrhea."

Dimitriou asked, "And are you saying that he told you that on that night he gave her vitamin B-12 and meperidine for her nausea?"

Pease said, "That's correct."

Pease explained that he had thought he asked Gilmore if he told the district attorney that. He said he didn't remember any response. "At the time I didn't know what meperidine was. I'm still not sure that I know what meperidine is."

Pease said, however, that nothing Gilmore told him caused him any great alarm. He explained that Patty and Gilmore would have dinner at the Whit-Mar. He didn't recall them ever stopping in just for drinks. They would sit at the bar for drinks, then have dinner, and then have another drink at the bar. He said they were always friendly to each other.

Dimitriou asked, "And how would you describe Doctor Gilmore's condition on the 14th or 15th when this conversation was going on?"

Pease responded, "By the time we were ready to leave the Whit-Mar, Doc was very emotionally upset. Like I said, he had two drinks while we were there. I don't know what he had before that. You could tell that the alcohol was starting to take effect on him."

Dimitriou asked, "Did Doc say to you that he had ever given Patty any meperidine at any other time? Was there any discussion about any other injection?"

Pease replied, "Doc talked about giving Patty injections if she had been out and drank too much before, and then Doc would give her an injection then. My impression was that Patty regularly got sick if she had too much to drink, and then Doc would then give her an injection to straighten her out. Doc talked about vitamin B. I think he mentioned Lomotil, I think that is the name of it; maybe Demerol but I am not sure whether he mentioned that the night of the 14th or 15th or not."

Dimitriou questioned, "So on the 14th or 15th, he may have used the term Demerol, he had given her Demerol on other occasions—"

Pease responded, "Yes."

"—is that your recollection?"

Pease said that as well as he could remember, that was true.

Dimitriou wanted to know if Gilmore, when talking about the meperidine, referred to a specific time as far as meperidine was concerned. Pease said that during the conversation with him, his recollection was that the meperidine was with the vitamin B shots on the 26th or 27th.

Dimitriou asked, "That is the way you remember the conversation. And when he referred to that particular time, the 26th or 27th, your recollection is that he said meperidine and vitamin B-12?"

Pease said yes, and confirmed that when Gilmore referred to other occasions, he talked about Lomotil and he thought vitamin B again. And Demerol.

Dimitriou asked Pease if Gilmore was emotionally upset when he met with him on the 14th or 15th and the 22nd. Pease said that Gilmore was upset, and had cried on both occasions.

Dimitriou said, "I think you also made the statement that Doc, on the 14th or 15th, said to you that he didn't think he had killed Patty?"

Pease responded that Gilmore did say that, and that he also said if he had thought he had killed Patty, he wasn't sure he could live with himself.

That is when the conversation about the gun came up, and led to the events mentioned earlier about giving the gun to Barry Gilmore.

Dimitriou asked, "Did he tell you what time it was that he gave her this injection?"

Pease said he didn't recall.

Dimitriou followed up, "Did he say to you that he thought he might have given her such an injection or that he could have?"

Pease said, "My recollection of that conversation is that Doc told me he gave her this injection of meperidine and vitamin B."

Dimitriou changed the subject. "By the way, with regard to the syringe and the swab which you have testified to, he told you, on December the 22nd, that he had thrown those away that morning of November 27th, right?"

Pease said that he didn't tell him anything about the syringe or swab other than the fact that he threw them away. He did say that Gilmore told him there was blood on the cotton swab.

At the conclusion of the testimony given on the two days the preliminary hearing was held, District Judge Henry Schultz ordered Gilmore held for trial.

Chapter
11

The Slow Journey
to Justice Begins

Doctor Gilmore waived arraignment on October 23, 1981, in Berks County Court on charges of criminal homicide, recklessly endangering the life of another, and aggravated assault, all charges related to the death of Patricia Gilmore the previous year on Thanksgiving Day. Police say that the doctor beat his wife and then gave her fatal injections of the drug meperidine, commonly known as Demerol.

An arraignment is a proceeding at which a person charged with a crime is informed of the charge against him and is asked to enter a plea. During the arraignment, the person charged appears before a judge in a courtroom, at which time the reading of the criminal charge or charges against this defendant takes place.

A defendant can then plead "guilty," "not guilty," or "no contest" to the charges filed against him. If a "not guilty" plea is entered the judge will set a date for the trial, and in some cases the date for the preliminary hearing. At this time the judge may change the bail amount based on the various factors of the case.

The judge is not required to automatically accept a guilty plea in a homicide case, but may instead schedule a hearing. During this hearing, the judge will review the seriousness and other elements of the crime, and the defendant's situation, and then schedule dates for the future proceedings.

When waiving arraignment the defendant acknowledges that he has been informed of and understands the charge against him and is willing to cede the formal arraignment proceeding.

During the coming long months, Gilmore was allowed to remain free on $50,000 bail. Dimitriou used the time to develop a defense strategy, a main ingredient appearing to be the intentional slowing down of the case's progression down the legal road to the inevitable criminal trial.

The Muhlenberg Police continued their investigation of Patty's death, using the time to search for any facts related to the tragedy they might have missed, and to tighten up any weak points in their case.

During this time, special prosecutor Charles Haddad also did his preparation. Haddad was doing the job that District Attorney George Yatron would normally have been doing before disqualifying himself and his staff from handling the case due to a conflict of interest—Yatron's reason was that he and his staff knew Doctor Gilmore while Gilmore served as a deputy coroner.

The prosecutor is typically responsible for deciding what the specific charges against the defendant will be, and what he will stand trial for. He has the job of pursuing a conviction, convincing a judge or jury that the defendant is guilty of the crime he has been charged with. Haddad needed to build his case using the available evidence and testimony. He also had to concentrate on jury selection. Sympathy among potential jury members would be high for Gilmore, who was known as a doctor beloved by his patients because they knew he sincerely cared for them. Also, he had always displayed a willingness to help make his community a better place to live. An opinion shared by most people is that doctors tend to have higher standards of character and morality because of the years of dedication and sacrifice it takes while studying to become a physician, and then to work in this challenging and demanding profession.

Among the greatest impact the prosecutor personally has in any capital case is deciding what degree of charge the defendant will be tried for. The higher the degree the more severe the punishment will usually be. The prosecutor is also in a position to pleabargain with the defendant and his attorney. Lesser degrees normally result in a lighter sentence. In many hard-to-prove cases a prosecutor is willing to settle for a lighter punishment in return for a guaranteed conviction. That is also true when the prosecutor feels he is going to have a difficult time finding a jury that is not emotionally charged in favor of the defendant, which could easily be surmised in the Gilmore case.

Springtime 1982 arrived without any word of the Gilmore murder case. Muhlenberg Police claimed that they had convinced the state attorney general's office to file the charges the previous October. However, apparently nothing was being done about the charges against Glosser, which included falsifying official records and obstruction of justice. News accounts stated that the attorney general's office didn't believe there was enough evidence to charge Glosser, but reportedly the Muhlenberg Police believed they had all the evidence they needed to take action.

Then county judge Forrest Schaeffer Jr. approved a continuance of Gilmore's June 2, 1982, pretrial hearing. Both Haddad and Dimitriou had requested the delay.

In the state of Pennsylvania, a pretrial hearing takes place after a defendant's preliminary hearing. Evidence and testimony presented at the preliminary hearing determine whether there is enough evidence to have a trial. The prosecution and the defense use the pretrial hearing to present motions to the county judge. This pretrial phase, commonly known as motion practice, is filed mainly in paper form.

There are many motions that may be made during this pretrial process. Some motions include asking the judge to: exclude evidence, exclude the defendant's statements or confession, grant access to evidence in the possession of the prosecution, compel or exclude testimony from certain people, require the opposing party to release evidence, and to dismiss the case or relocate the trial.

On November 5, 1982, another delay tactic was handed up onto the judicial field of play. Judge Schaeffer, displeased with being required to make the ruling, agreed to continue Gilmore's trial, scheduled to begin November 15, until early the following year. Muhlenberg Police Chief Smith said later that the delay was ridiculous and that he and Detective Hadley had not been asked for any input concerning the aspects of the case, including agreeing to the continuance.

Smith and Hadley noted that two years had gone by since Patricia Gilmore's death, and reminded everyone that as time goes by witnesses' recollections are going to become faded, and it will be more difficult to track down key witnesses.

The new trial date was set for January 10, 1983, while Gilmore remained free on $50,000 bail. Schaeffer hesitated, but then agreed to the continuance after Haddad said he had no objection. Dimitriou claimed the reason for his delay request was the fact that the transcription of testimony taken during a September 3 preliminary hearing had just been transcribed that Thursday, certainly not giving him sufficient time to review the testimony and prepare a formal defense presentation in court. Dimitriou had entered pretrial requests for the suppression of three statements Gilmore made to police, alleging that the statements were obtained illegally.

Judge Schaeffer questioned why it took so long to get the hearing's testimony transcribed, considering the preliminary hearing was held in early September. An additional ingredient to the misadventure of delays was Dimitriou telling the court that he was representing a lawyer from another county accused of misconduct and would be required later in the month to appear before the Pennsylvania Disciplinary Board of the Supreme Court. Dimitriou reminded Schaeffer that such hearings have priority over any other legal matters. Schaeffer told Dimitriou that if Gilmore's trial would have started November 15, it could easily have been recessed for a day or two to allow for his presence at the disciplinary board hearings. To insure that there won't be further delays, Schaeffer ordered Dimitriou to present his briefs to the court no later than November 30.

Dimitriou, trying to get the arrest overturned on technicalities and suppressed evidence, had been able to get two delays. Scheduled to start in August, it was postponed to November 5, and now it was being pushed back to January 10, 1983, more that two years after the alleged crime took place.

Gilmore had waived the Pennsylvania 180-day rule, which requires prosecutors to bring a case to trial within 180 days. Defendants that waive the rule do so to give their lawyers time to prepare a defense. Unfortunately, when the waiver is given, it makes frequent delays and postponements possible.

Now the case seemed to be at an impasse. Legal minds will argue that prolonged delays, even if initiated by the defendant's own doing, could damage the defendant's case. These types of delays for sure make it tougher for the prosecution, as witnesses' memories fade and others disappear through normal moving around or dying. Complicated cases at the local, state, and federal level get done well within the 180-day period. The big question then is why couldn't the Gilmore case progress at a normal pace? Was asking for delays just a part of Manny Dimitriou's plan of defense?

Meanwhile, the Glosser case was heating up. On November 23, 1982, Muhlenberg Police filed obstruction of justice and tampering with public records charges against Doctor Glosser. They accused the now former county coroner of covering up damaging evidence in the death of his friend and fellow doctor's wife. When it was time to set a date for his preliminary hearing, District Judge Doris Dorminy, who had jurisdiction, recused herself from presiding over it, stating that she personally knew Glosser and Gilmore. Dorminy had also recused herself from the Gilmore case, resulting in District Judge Schultz presiding over this hearing.

As of December 13, court administrators had not yet assigned a district judge to preside at Glosser's preliminary hearing. District Attorney George Yatron said that because no judge had been selected, no hearing date had been set.

Police alleged that Glosser, while serving as coroner, covered up the drug-injection death of Patricia Gilmore by ruling it an accident, death resulting from her choking on her own vomit. While Reading Hospital pathologist Doctor John Keith was performing the autopsy, Glosser instructed him to halt testing of tissue samples. Despite Glosser's orders, Keith ordered further tests that allegedly discovered meperidine as the cause of death,

Glosser's lawyer, William Bernhart, wrote Yatron asking him to withdraw from prosecuting the Glosser case, just as he did with the Gilmore case, because staff members knew the defendant. That, of course, is what caused Charles Haddad to be appointed special prosecutor by the state attorney general's office. Yatron announced that he wouldn't withdraw from prosecuting Glosser. He saw no conflict, because Glosser no longer held office and staff members who knew him no longer worked in the district attorney's office.

As expected, print and broadcast media coverage was

ramped up as the trial date approached. The local press reported that defense lawyer Emmanuel Dimitriou made a last-ditch
attempt to have the murder case dismissed. He argued on January 7, 1983, in Berks County Court, just three days before trial,
that no incriminating evidence exists against his client. Judge
Schaeffer had said he would render his decision on Monday,
January 10, just prior to the trial's scheduled start. Dimitriou
insisted that Schaeffer dismiss all charges against Gilmore. He
was quoted, "There is no direct evidence whatsoever—there
is no motive. There is no evidence of threats, no evidence of
abuse, no evidence of arguments, no evidence of altercations."

But Special Prosecutor Charles Haddad pointed out to
Schaeffer that State Trooper Barrie Pease testified under oath
that Gilmore told him he gave his wife an injection of meperidine. Dimitriou said that because there were four to six
fresh hypodermic needle marks found on her buttocks during
the autopsy, the one shot that Gilmore said he gave her meant
nothing considering that the prosecution can't produce anyone
who can testify as to who was responsible for each of the other
needle marks.

Dimitriou repeated a previous contention that Patty Gilmore might have injected herself. He said that she had gone into
Gilmore's medical bag on previous occasions, and there is reason to believe she was capable of giving herself a shot.

Dimitriou reminded the judge that Gilmore had also told
Pease he gave Patty an injection of vitamin B along with the
meperidine because her stomach was upset, and there is no evidence as to the potency of that meperidine dose or whether the
amount of the drug found in her blood during the autopsy was
sufficient to cause death.

Dimitriou also argued that bruises found on the corpse

could have been caused by a number of falls, and that there's no evidence that Doctor Gilmore caused any of them.

Haddad contended that Gilmore's change in stories caused suspicion. He said Gilmore denied when being questioned by police that he had injected Patty with anything, but later told Pease that he injected her with vitamin B and meperidine.

Haddad noted that the amount of meperidine found in Patty's blood far exceeded any normal dosage, and there was no medical reason for that amount of meperidine to be injected into the victim. Dismissing Dimitriou's claim that the victim could have injected herself, he reminded Schaeffer that Gilmore had thrown away a hypodermic needle and a wad of cotton that had blood on it.

On Monday, January 10, Judge Schaeffer turned down defense motions to dismiss the case and rejected defense claims that there wasn't enough evidence against Gilmore to warrant a trial.

Schaeffer also rejected the defense's motion to suppress statements Gilmore gave during his lengthy interrogation by Muhlenberg Police without a lawyer present, and also the conversations he had with Trooper Barry Pease.

After Schaeffer announced his rulings he initiated the process, along with Haddad and Dimitriou, of selecting a jury for a trial that could easily last a month, possibly longer. Dimitriou obviously felt that the prosecution's case was strong enough to get a jury to convict his client of criminal homicide, aggravated assault, and recklessly endangering another person. Conviction would most certainly mean a long prison sentence.

The jury selection task was short lived, however. Just as the trial process was about to begin, Gilmore pleaded guilty to involuntary manslaughter. Dimitriou used the Alford plea to en-

ter his client's plea. A rare type of guilty plea set by legal precedent and upheld by appeals court decisions, this plea process
allows a defendant to enter a plea of guilty without admitting
to committing the crime. In this way he is in a stronger position
to negotiate for a more lenient sentence. Dimitriou stated that
Gilmore's memory is blank when trying to recall what happened on that Thanksgiving Day morning, mostly because he
was asleep as a result of substantial alcohol consumption while
socializing the night before.

Schaeffer and Haddad agreed that Dimitriou could enter
the plea, but a source at the time reported that Schaeffer at
first balked, wondering how a defendant can plead guilty to a
charge without admitting to the crime. He insisted that Gilmore
specifically admit killing his wife, but he changed his mind after reviewing the three appellate cases Dimitriou cited stating
that a plea lacking that specific admission was permissible. The
courts ruled in opinions handed down in 1969 by the state Supreme Court, by the U.S. Supreme Court in 1970, and in 1973
by the state Superior Court, that such pleas are permissible.

While the details were not disclosed to the public, the local media reported that some confidential sources gave away
the plea conditions: Doctor Gilmore would serve five years of
probation and work a certain amount of predetermined hours
performing community service.

A charge of involuntary manslaughter, which is a first-
degree misdemeanor, carries a maximum prison term of five
years and a maximum fine of $10,000. Gilmore also faced the
possibility of losing his state medical license.

Of course, this whole plea deal hinged on getting Judge
Schaeffer's blessing. He would make his decision at the time
of sentencing. Meanwhile, he ordered Gilmore to undergo psy-

chiatric testing and a thorough physical examination, and directed the Berks County probation office to conduct a complete presentence background investigation.

The issue was Gilmore pleading guilty despite his claim that he remembered nothing about what happened and therefore cannot admit to committing the slaying or participating in any role in it. Dimitriou said Gilmore's lack of memory was due to the influence of alcohol plus physical exhaustion. The claim was made despite Gilmore's revealing details about that Thanksgiving Day and the night before while being interrogated by Muhlenberg Police, and during the conversations he had with Trooper Barrie Pease.

Gilmore appeared before Judge Schaeffer for sentencing on February 28, at which time Schaeffer refused to accept the plea and ordered the doctor to stand trial. Schaeffer gave the reason for turning down the plea as Dimitriou balking at permitting Gilmore to answer questions concerning what the doctor remembered about the night of the death of his wife. Judge Schaeffer particularly wanted to ask Gilmore to explain how he could tell Trooper Pease days after Patty's death that he gave her injections of meperidine and vitamin B but now claim he doesn't have any memory of what happened. Dimitriou said these questions were irrelevant, maintaining that his client was being subjected to double jeopardy since Gilmore had already asserted in his plea that he did not remember what happened.

Refuting Dimitriou's double-jeopardy argument, Haddad later said the facts of what happened do not legally support Dimitriou's contention.

Dimitriou and Haddad had reached an unofficial plea agreement calling for Gilmore to be sentenced to five years probation and fined $5,000 and ordered to do some kind of community medical work. That deal fell apart when Schaeffer refused to accept the guilty plea.

What the Gilmore case and the Alford case and two companion cases had in common were that the defendants had all pleaded guilty to charges while not specifically admitting they committed their crimes. There was a significant difference, however, between the Gilmore case and the three others. In the Gilmore case the guilty plea was being entered before sentencing, while each of the other three defendants had filed appeals to modify their pleas and have their convictions overturned. These cases, despite all three being unsuccessful, gave Dimitriou the legal precedent he needed to cite the cases when entering his plea as it applied to the Gilmore case. The high courts had ruled that even though the defendants had entered their guilty pleas freely with a full understanding of all the possible repercussions, the three lost their arguments in separate appellate cases because they had, unlike Doctor Irvin Gilmore, already been sentenced.

Dimitriou considered the 1969 state Supreme Court decision to be the most applicable to the Gilmore case because of the similarities of the victim's death and the legal pleading. The most famous of the cases involved an appeal to the highest court in the land, the U.S. Supreme Court by Harry Alford. Alford pleaded guilty in 1963 to a charge of second-degree murder and was sentenced in North Carolina to be incarcerated for thirty years. Alford chose to plead guilty to second-degree murder rather than be tried for first-degree murder and risk being sentenced to death. While entering the guilty plea he insisted that he was innocent and that the only reason he was pleading guilty was fear of being sentenced to death. In his appeal he claimed that by being coerced into entering the guilty plea his constitutional rights had been violated. Alford lost his appeal. In its issuing opinion the court added that Alford came to realize that he had a choice of either risking his life by going to trial or pleading guilty and receiving a maximum thirty-year prison sentence. Avoiding a trial was his safe bet, considering the overwhelming evidence against him. In 1965 Thomas Cottrell, who pleaded guilty to homicide in Philadelphia, insisted he didn't recall anything about the stabbing of his wife. He blamed his memory lapse on being intoxicated. Cottrell was convicted and sentenced to ten to twenty years in prison. In his appeal Cottrell stated his guilty plea should be thrown out because he could not remember the crime. The state Supreme Court rejected that argument.

In the third case, James Shank pleaded guilty in 1971 to a morals charge. In his appeal he contended that the plea should be disallowed because he didn't fully admit to the crime. The Superior Court disagreed, noting that even though he never fully admitted his guilt he had never fully denied involvement in the crime.

District Attorney George Yatron had requested that the state attorney general take over the prosecuting of Doctor Glosser. Yatron had the same fears that he did when the possibility of prosecuting Gilmore came up—staff members in his office were too familiar with Doctor Glosser, having worked with him while he served as acting coroner. Yatron was understandably concerned that these relationships could cause a higher court to grant a new trial or even overturn Glosser's conviction of lying on Patty Gilmore's death certificate and tampering with public records and obstructing justice.

Yatron patiently waited for any word from the attorney general's office. He knew that if that office opted out he'd be on the hook to try the case in spite of the conflict-of-interest issues. Particularly alarming was Glosser's lawyer, William Bernhart, who also objected to Yatron handling the case, declaring that he intended to call some district attorney's office staff members as witnesses. Yatron was convinced that his staff members being called as witnesses for the defense while at the same time serving as prosecutors would surely jeopardize his chances of getting a jury to hand down guilty verdicts, and it would pour gasoline on the fire heating up the defendant's inevitable appeal efforts.

Despite Yatron's pleas, Zimmerman turned down his request for a special prosecutor, convinced that Yatron would be able to provide a prosecutor who was not a staff member while Glosser was acting coroner.

Yatron, having no choice in the matter, then proceeded to name an assistant to prosecute Glosser. Yatron's concerns were soon validated, however, as a result of Judge Schaeffer issuing an order on March 15, 1983, disqualifying the district attorney's office from prosecuting Glosser. In his ruling Schaeffer agreed with Bernhard that there would exist a conflict of interest if Yatron's office handled the case. Schaeffer, as president judge, had the authority to request intervention by the attorney general's office, which then at that point agreed to appoint a special prosecutor.

Meanwhile, back on March 8, a week after Schaeffer rejected the guilty plea on February 28, Dimitriou had thrown another kitchen sink into the drama. He filed a petition claiming that Schaeffer was prejudiced against Gilmore and asked that the jurist remove himself from the case. Schaeffer denied that petition.

On March 10 Dimitriou continued his legal fusillade. Citing expansive publicity received as a result of official disclosure and the media's coverage of it, he asked the Berks County court for a change of venue for the trial. In his petition Dimitriou reported that special prosecutor Haddad also agreed that the case should be moved.

Schaeffer scheduled a hearing and acted quickly. On March 13 he granted Gilmore a change in venue. It was a guaranteed six-month delay in the start of the trial. The state Supreme Court was charged with deciding where the trial would be held. Haddad and Dimitriou both wanted the trial moved to another county rather than bringing out-of-county jurors to Reading for trial in the Berks County courthouse.

Schaeffer conceded that the public had strong feelings about the case and bought Dimitriou's claim that public opinion in Berks was decidedly anti-Gilmore, mostly because of the media coverage of Schaefer's denial of Gilmore's guilty plea with five years of probation.

On June 2, State Supreme Court Justice William Hutchinson refused Dimitriou's request to postpone the long-delayed trial until a hearing could be held before the Supreme Court to remove Schaeffer as presiding judge. In Dimitriou's request to have Schaeffer removed from the case, he stated in his petition that Schaeffer was not sitting as an impartial judge and was prejudiced against his client, siding repeatedly in petition rulings with the prosecution. Dimitriou also contended that Schaeffer bowed to public opinion when rejecting the defense's double-jeopardy pleas. Hutchinson ruled that any such hearing could be held following the trial as grounds for an appeal if Gilmore is found guilty. In refusing Dimitriou's request, Hutchinson scheduled the trial to start Monday, June 6, in the Schuylkill County Courthouse in Pottsville, Pennsylvania, about 35 miles north of Berks County's seat, Reading, Pennsylvania.

On Friday afternoon, June 3, Dimitriou filed an appeal of a decision made earlier that day by Schaeffer. At that hearing Dimitriou again pleaded the double-jeopardy argument and reminded Schaeffer that he had accepted Gilmore pleading guilty January 10, 1983, to an involuntary manslaughter charge and scheduled sentencing for February 28. Dimitriou claimed that as a result of his entering a guilty plea that past January 10, Gilmore cannot be made to face the charges again. Dimitriou argued that if Gilmore was forced to face charges it would be double jeopardy.

Schaeffer turned down the defense request to dismiss the case on double-jeopardy grounds. Schaeffer's reason was Dimitriou's refusal to allow Gilmore to answer the court's questions about the night of Patty Gilmore's death. Dimitriou claimed that his client was exhausted and intoxicated the night of Patty's death and couldn't remember anything.

Dimitriou had prepared all the paperwork in advance just in case he would need to file an immediate appeal to the Superior Court if Schaeffer rejected the guilty plea; such an appeal would delay the start of the trial by as long as two years.

Dimitriou had indicated that if the Superior Court turned down his appeal, he would appeal to the state Supreme Court; doing that of course would further delay the trial. The facts were that a trial could be scheduled only if Dimitriou eventually lost all his appeals.

On June 28, 1983, the Pennsylvania Supreme Court turned down Dimitriou's petition to have Schaeffer removed from the case as presiding judge. The court said it would not review defense allegations that Judge Schaeffer was biased against Doctor Gilmore. That decision was handed down fairly quickly.

That would not be the case with Dimitriou's double-jeopardy appeal of Schaeffer's ruling. A ruling on Dimitriou's appeal to the state Superior Court could be a long time coming. Waiting for a ruling on that complicated legal appeal was expected to delay Gilmore's already delayed trial for two years or longer. Dimitriou's appeal contended that the case against Gilmore should be dismissed on double-jeopardy grounds. Dimitriou said Gilmore's guilty plea was a conviction, and therefore he cannot, because of constitutional protection against double jeopardy, be required to face the same charges again.

On December 8, 1983, Dimitriou and Haddad argued their cases before a three-member panel of Superior Court judges. Haddad countered Dimitriou's claims, stating that the prosecution contends that a conviction only legally exists after a defendant is sentenced, which Gilmore was not. That three-judge panel's decision rejecting Dimitriou's contentions was issued on June 22, 1984. Dimitriou then asked the full Superior Court to reconsider the decision.

The media reported on September 4, 1984, that the entire state Superior Court in Philadelphia had refused to consider a second appeal to dismiss the murder charges. Dimitriou right away said he would appeal the case to the state Supreme Court within the next month. That court too, according to April 27, 1985, news reports, refused to consider the double-jeopardy appeal.

An intruding sidebar to the continuing Gilmore saga emerged as the new year 1986 got underway. The weeklong trial of Doctor William Glosser ended Friday afternoon, January 24, 1986, with a deadlocked jury. The jury, made up of seven men and five women, split 6–6 after deliberating for over six hours. The trial had been moved from Berks County to next-door Lancaster County because of extensive pretrial publicity.

Glosser, a close friend of Gilmore's, was serving as acting Berks County coroner when Patty Gilmore died. He was accused of covering up the true cause of her death, willfully altering a death certificate, and obstructing justice. Lancaster County Senior Judge Wilson Bucher, who was the presiding judge, dismissed the first charge during the trial, citing lack of evidence.

Prosecutors had claimed that Glosser willfully signed a death certificate he knew was erroneous when he stated that Patty died by choking on her vomit and was classified as an accidental death.

Bucher didn't have any choice but to declare a mistrial after the jury reported they could not reach a unanimous decision. According to press reports one juror said he had thought there was enough evidence to convict the 75-year-old doctor but there were jurors that believed otherwise. Reportedly, some or all of the jurors noticed that the cause of death listed on the death certificate included the words "in the opinion of " preceding it. Evidently those words led six members to conclude that a death certificate was not the final disposition in declaring how someone died.

This same juror, while being interviewed by the news media, said the deliberations were frustrating because the case was so complicated. There were a lot of missing pieces, he said. "It's frustrating to spend five days and not come up with a decision." The juror also said that Bucher's dismissal of the one charge might have added to the confusion. The attempt by defense counsel to discredit Doctor John Keith, who performed the autopsy of Patricia Gilmore's body, had not been successful, the juror said. Quoted in interviews, the juror said, "We thought Keith was a fine pathologist."

Meanwhile, the star prosecution witness on Monday, the opening day of Glosser's trial, was none other than Keith, 50, who, while testifying, disclosed that he had filed a civil lawsuit in U. S. District Court in Philadelphia in November charging that the Reading Hospital and nine individuals, including hospital officials, other doctors, and politicians, conspired to have him fired because he refused to help with an alleged cover-up of the real cause of Patty Gilmore's death. In the suit Keith asked for damages of more that $10,000. The doctor had recently accepted a position with Pottsville (Pennsylvania) Hospital as an assistant pathologist.

News reports said Keith accused the hospital and the individuals of eleven charges including racketeering, civil rights violations, violating his right of free speech, antitrust violations, wrongful firing, breach of contract, breach of good-faith dealing, interfering with lawful business activities, defamation of character, inflicting emotional distress, and fraud.

Keith's testimony at Glosser's trial was basically a rehash of what he said at Gilmore's preliminary hearing. He had found bruises and needle marks on the body, and was denied his request to have a police officer present during the autopsy.

Keith discovered a high level of meperidine (brand name Demerol), a narcotic depressant. He said Glosser tried to talk him out of sending blood samples to an outside laboratory to determine the amount of the drug in the body. The laboratory results showed lethal levels of the drug, plus alcohol.

While these findings were being established, Glosser signed a death certificate listing the cause of death as accidental, choking on her stomach's contents.

Following his testifying at the Gilmore preliminary hearing, Keith said Glosser stopped assigning the coroner's office autopsies to him, depriving him of a source of income. Keith also said that hospital officials suggested he resign, implying that if someone else had done the Gilmore autopsy the hospital wouldn't be having the problems it was being forced to deal with. Keith also claimed that Glosser ordered him not to give the results of toxicological studies to police.

Finally, Keith claimed that in December of 1983 officials at the hospital asked for his resignation. They told him that if he didn't resign he would be fired.

Over a year after the state Supreme Court refused to consider the double-jeopardy appeal, Manny Dimitriou was notified that a three-member panel of the U.S. Third Circuit Court of Appeals also rejected his double-jeopardy claim. On June 30, 1986, he said he might request that all 10 members of the appeals court hear the appeal, explaining that one of the cases he had presented to the panel was later reversed by another circuit court panel, thus creating a conflict. He claimed that conflict could be resolved by having the entire appeals court review the Gilmore case. He also said it was possible he would bypass the circuit court altogether and petition the U.S. Supreme Court to hear the case. He said he wouldn't decide what his next legal move would be until he reviewed the panel's entire written opinion.

Dimitriou continued to contend that Gilmore's 1983 open guilty plea to a charge of involuntary manslaughter was the same as a conviction. An open guilty plea leaves the sentencing up to the judge instead of setting a prior agreed-upon sentence in a plea bargain. Judge Schaeffer had earlier rejected a plea-bargain agreement consisting of a sentence of five years of probation and community service, but he did accept the open guilty plea along with the opportunity to question Gilmore about the case. Dimitriou objected to the questioning, resulting in Schaeffer throwing out the guilty plea and ordering Gilmore to stand trial.

On July 16 Dimitriou did what was expected—he asked the entire Third U.S. Circuit Court to hear the double-jeopardy appeal. Less than two weeks later he once again was dealt a legal rejection. The circuit court turned down his request to have the entire court hear the appeal.

On September 29, 1986, he continued the long legal battle when he filed a petition asking the highest court in the land, the U.S. Supreme Court, to rule on whether Gilmore's constitutional rights against being tried twice for the same crime would be violated if he were brought to trial.

Chapter
12

The Trial

February 1987 arrived. Appeals and petitions had been exhausted, a jury had been selected, and witnesses gathered. Finally it was time for the trial of Doctor Irvin Gilmore, charged with killing his wife, Patricia Ann Gilmore, a trial that never would have been had Judge Forrest Schaeffer allowed the doctor to plead guilty to involuntary manslaughter over four years earlier. Schaeffer, a capable and tested jurist, would only accept the plea deal if Gilmore explained how he could tell Trooper Pease days after Patty's death that he gave her injections of meperidine and vitamin B but later claim he didn't have any memory of what happened that Thanksgiving eve. Dimitriou turned down Schaeffer's requirement that Gilmore testify.

Every morning a rendezvous between an older man and younger woman was taking place on the parking lot of the state police barracks in Hamburg, Pennsylvania. These weren't clandestine meetings—the two were meeting for strictly business reasons.

Berks County's official court reporter Karen Moran would travel north fifteen miles from Reading, and Berks County president judge Schaeffer would drive west from his northern Berks County home. They would then carpool and drive the twenty or so miles north on Route 61 to the Schuylkill County courthouse in Pottsville, Pennsylvania, to hold the murder trial moved there after Schaeffer approved a change of venue petition. Schaeffer's job was to sit as the presiding judge, and Moran would be transcribing every word spoken.

Pottsville, located in the heart of the Pennsylvania anthracite coal region, was the hometown of famed novelist John O'Hara. It was laid out on steep hills and deep hollows. It was a town with sharp geographical edges and public opinions to match.

Gilmore, charged with criminal homicide, aggravated assault, and recklessly endangering another person would be defended at trial by his highly skilled attorney Emmanuel Dimitriou, who had been on the case since the beginning. However, Charles Mackin, Jr., chief deputy attorney general, now would be leading the prosecution, replacing Charles Haddad.

The entire case against Gilmore was now going to be played out like a spectacular drama projected on the silver screen of a movie house or on the boards of a Broadway theater. Every detail, every bit of testimony, and every medical test was going to be rehashed during the following days, and then presented to a jury that would seal the fate of the doctor. The courtroom story began with Patty's death that Thanksgiving morning, then his interview with Muhlenberg Police without benefit of legal counsel, continued with Doctor Gilmore's confiding discussions with Trooper Barrie Pease, the charges presented against him, all of the revealing testimony at the preliminary hearing, the years of legal wrangling by Emmanuel Dimitriou, and now the recounting and revelations of a large group of characters—a cast made up of family, friends, neighbors, police investigators, medical experts, and of course lawyers.

The prosecution claimed that Patricia Gilmore had been dead for hours before her body was discovered in the Gilmore home on November 27, 1980, and, more importantly, the body had been moved before ambulance attendants and a Muhlenberg Police officer arrived.

Police shortly after charged Gilmore with injecting Patricia that morning or the evening before with a fatal dose of meperidine, known by the brand name Demerol. When it was combined with the large amount of alcohol in her system, it caused her death.

The defense, explaining that Gilmore is a doctor who still

makes house calls, had often left his medical bag in the back seat of his car. Dimitriou contended that Patty Gilmore easily could have taken the bag out of the car during the night, and then injected herself in the buttocks. Charles Mackin didn't see it that way. He maintained that Doctor Gilmore injected his wife with the lethal dosage, and Mackin claimed that Patty was too drunk to inject herself in the buttocks. He pointed out to the jury that she had a blood-alcohol level of 0.24, and emphasized that in Pennsylvania a person is intoxicated with a blood-alcohol level of 0.10 or above.

Dimitriou countered with defense witness Louise Holland, a patient of Gilmore's, who testified she had seen Patricia Gilmore inject herself in the buttocks at the doctor's office. That, coupled with the fact that Dimitriou had doctors scheduled to testify that bruises on the body noted during the autopsy could have occurred after death, seemed to get the defense started on an incontrovertible course.

The Gilmores might have had a reasonably sustainable marriage, but it was, like most marriages, certainly not idyllic—their lifestyle was fueled by alcohol and prescription drugs. Doctor Larry Rotenberg, director of psychiatry at Reading Hospital, testified that he saw Patty Gilmore on May 30, 1978, at 2:30 a.m. in the hospital emergency room for anxiety issues following what he described as domestic problems complicated by the consumption of alcohol. He said she wanted to be admitted to the hospital, although he didn't feel it was really necessary. In the morning she was embarrassed when she found herself in the psychiatric ward. She left the hospital immediately after Doctor Gilmore came and got her without receiving any medical treatment or following normal discharge procedures.

Registered nurse Arlene Meas wrote in her report that night

that Mrs. Gilmore was there for "protection from a threatening home situation." Meas, reading from the report from the witness stand, noted that Mrs. Gilmore said she was allergic to vitamin B, among other things.

Nancy Hoeffer, a friend of Patty's, testified Patty told her she took Demerol occasionally because she liked the feeling. Hoeffer said that at night on October 16, 1980, she saw Patty in a local bar. Hoeffer said her friend didn't appear intoxicated, but was very upset and kept saying her husband hated her. About 10:30 p.m. the two of them went to Hoeffer's house, and later Patty called Gilmore to come and get her. She told Hoeffer he refused, at which time Hoeffer called him and asked him to come and pick up his wife. She said Gilmore said he was too tired to go anywhere. The next day, Hoeffer said Doctor Gilmore phoned and asked if she had found a ring Patty thought she had left at her house.

Hoeffer didn't have contact with Patty again until November 25, 1980, when Hoeffer called and told Patty she wanted to learn CPR. Patty replied that she was not conducting CPR classes again until springtime.

Dimitriou, while cross-examining her, pointed out that Hoeffer's testimony had some clear discrepancies. He said that in a previous statement she had said that Patty Gilmore was fairly intoxicated when she visited her house October 16, 1980, and that Patty called Hoeffer about the ring, not Doctor Gilmore.

There were many conflicting accounts about the relationship between Doctor Gilmore and his wife, including information given in the statement Gilmore made December 11, 1980, to Stuart Suss, at the time an assistant district attorney, Muhlenberg Police Chief Harley Smith, and Muhlenberg Police Officers Kermit Frantz and Barry Hadley. He had said he never knew his wife to inject herself, but she could have: "If you have ever been in the dressing room, there is a full-length mirror that takes two-thirds of the wall, so I'm sure if she did try to inject herself with the lights on, she would certainly have a full view."

In his statement to Suss, Gilmore did repeat that Patty was afraid of Demerol—it made her sick. She would have taken Stadol for her headaches. He had said she had been taking Lomotil because she had been suffering from diarrhea for nine days.

Continuing, he once again said that he and his wife often fell on the steps. It was not unusual for her to wake up with a bruise and not know how she got it.

And finally in his statement to Suss, he explained that the liquid found in the syringe could have been vitamin B complex, because he would give her that to fight off her nausea. Three packets, each containing thirty Lomotil tablets, were missing from his bag. Using his knowledge as a doctor, he said tests on Lomotil in the body will produce results similar to that of meperidine.

Gilmore's son Barry and his wife Linda, both schoolteachers, traveled from their Florida home to Pennsylvania for a typical holiday visit and family reunion, arriving on November 26, the day before Thanksgiving. Linda testified at the trial. She told about Patty picking them up at the airport, stopping at a gift shop to make a purchase, and then resting at the Gilmore home until it was time to go to have an Italian dinner of spaghetti and meatballs at the home of the Amoroso family, long-time friends of the doctor. Linda said she didn't recall anything about anybody's drinking before they left for the Amorosos'—she didn't have any, but she supposed that her husband probably had a beer. Linda said that she, Barry, Patty, and Doctor Gilmore arrived at the Amorosos' about 7:30 p.m. and stayed until about 1:30 a.m. The visit included dinner, predinner cocktails, and after-dinner drinks. Linda recalled, "We drank before dinner, and we had wine with dinner. We marched around, just had fun, just had a good time marching around and laughing and so forth."

Linda didn't have any after-dinner drinks. She did recall that Patty had wine with dinner and then started drinking scotch. Linda wasn't paying attention—she didn't know how much scotch Patty drank, and she could not recall how many martinis, the doctor's drink of choice, he had, or for that matter how many drinks Barry Gilmore had. She did say that Patty didn't appear drunk—she drove home from the Amorosos to the Gilmore house.

"We went home. Irv went right to bed. He said he was tired. He went straight to bed. My husband, Barry, stayed down with Patty and I in the kitchen. She had a glass of beer. Barry went down—I think he went downstairs and got her a beer and came up and probably talked, I would say, no longer than fifteen minutes, and then he had a headache. He said he had a headache, and then he went upstairs. So Patty and I were downstairs talking for I guess around twenty minutes, twenty to thirty minutes. I was pregnant at the time so I was tired and, you know, decided to go up. I was, you know, very tired."

Linda testified that she and Patty talked about Thanksgiving dinner and the china she had bought for the occasion for about twenty minutes before Linda went upstairs about 2 a.m., leaving Patty alone in the kitchen. Linda, tired and exhausted, said she went straight to bed and didn't wake up until 8:30 a.m. Linda was awakened by the doctor talking to his son.

Mackin asked, "Okay. Can you recall what was being said at that time?"

Linda replied, "He said, 'Barry.' And he opened the door. Our door was closed, and he opened our door. And that woke me up. And he said, what happened to Patty? I think she's dead, something to that effect, you know."

She said that Barry got up very quickly and got dressed, she taking a little more time. She then walked into the hallway and saw Patty from the hallway in her room. Linda didn't go into the bedroom, and when asked, she said she saw a medical bag.

"I saw it going downstairs. I was following Barry around. I was dazed myself, so I was following him around. And on an occasion to go downstairs, I was in the hallway. And looking into her dressing room, I saw it on the floor by the lounge chair on my way downstairs."

Linda said she recognized the bag as Gilmore's, and that it was open when she noticed it on the floor.

Mackin asked, "Now, even though you had a fairly brief experience with Patricia Gilmore, did she ever tell you that she—or had you ever seen her give herself an injection?"

Linda Gilmore's response was, "No."

Mackin asked about any bruises Linda might have noticed on Patty's body. She said that she didn't see any bruises.

Dimitriou wanted to know more about Patty picking Barry and Linda up at the airport.

"Let me ask you, when you got home before you went to the Amorosos' and when Patty picked you up, what was her attitude? I mean, how was she behaving? Did she seem upset about anything? Was she complaining about Irv, I mean, about the doc?"

Linda replied, "Not at all, very good spirits."

In fact, Linda testified that Gilmore was also in good spirits, happy to see his son and daughter-in-law. She indicated that nobody was upset with anybody, and nobody was complaining about anybody.

Dimitriou wanted to know more about the Amorosos' reputation for unusual social entertaining, consisting of marching around the room, hands on hips, singing, creating music and marching to it, telling jokes, holding hands and forming a line like the Mexican hat dance. Mr. Amoroso was known to recite, whenever he got a few drinks in him, "Gunga Din" or Rudyard Kipling.

Dimitriou asked, "And everybody was in good spirits?"

Linda replied, "Right."

"Nobody was arguing with anybody?"

She confirmed, "No."

Dimitriou asked, "Now, was she—was there anything unusual about her driving that would cause you to take notice of it?"

Linda responded, "I didn't notice anything. I was sitting in the back seat with my husband. And I didn't notice anything that I would have, you know, said to her, slow down or whatever. It was to me."

He asked, "She was driving okay?" Linda confirmed that.

She responded to his question as to whether she noticed Gilmore's medical bag on the back seat or elsewhere in the vehicle. She said she didn't see the medical bag in the vehicle.

Dimitriou asked if Patty complained about Gilmore when just they two were chatting in the kitchen.

Linda said, "No. In fact, we were talking about being pregnant at the time. We were talking about the baby and the flight up and just—"

Inez DiGiamberardino, the Gilmores' next-door neighbor, told Dimitriou that she was busy in her kitchen until 2:30 a.m. Thanksgiving eve, preparing for the holiday meal she would be serving the next day. She said about ten minutes after she went upstairs to prepare to go to bed she heard the door to the Gilmores' garage that led to the patio. She explained that the door always made a "thump" sound when it was pulled shut—she had heard it many times.

Inez DiGiamberardino explained that she had acute hearing. "Well, I don't see very well and I have compensated by listening much more carefully than maybe other people would."

She also recalled hearing Patty Gilmore call out to the Gilmore dogs. She said she was sure it was Patty's voice, and after speaking to the dogs it became quiet and she heard no more.

DiGiamberardino contacted the police after Patty's death.

Dimitriou asked her, "Mrs. DiGiamberardino, during the course of this investigation, did the police come to see you?"

She said they came to her house twice: the first time was right after the tragedy, and the second time was a few days later.

Dimitriou asked, "Did you take them up to your bedroom?"

She replied, "The second time. Officer Smith."

Dimitriou then changed his line of questioning, now focusing on an incident in May of 1978 when she accompanied Patty Gilmore to the hospital.

DiGiamberardino said, "She was distraught and she wanted to go to the hospital because she felt that she was being neglected and that Doctor Gilmore didn't spend enough time with her and his patients always came first." She continued, "Mrs. Gilmore told me that she had to teach Doc a lesson because his patients always came first before her."

Dimitriou asked, "She came over—did she come over to your house often?"

DiGiamberardino said Patty came to her house often and

they would sit and talk. "We'd have general conversations, about clothing or whatever women talk about when they get together."

Dimitriou asked, "Did she ever complain to you about Doctor Gilmore and the way he treated her other than the fact that his patients came first?"

"No. She was very proud of him."

"Tell me, that night, that night, did she complain to you about Doctor Gilmore abusing her in any way?"

DiGiamberardino responded, "No, she didn't."

Dimitriou asked, "Mrs. DiGiamberardino, did either Officer Hadley or Chief Smith call you a liar?"

Mackin objected to the question.

Schaeffer ruled, "Objection sustained. Now, Mr. Dimitriou, we went over that. That is absolutely irrelevant. Whatever attitude the police may have had is not material to this case."

After Mackin conducted a short cross-examination confirming that DiGiamberardino didn't hear Patty having a conversation with another person, Schaeffer asked her, "One question, Mrs. DiGiamberardino. When you saw Mrs. Gilmore on this night that she went to the hospital—were you able—and I understand you had some problem—were you able to see her?"

DiGiamberardino replied, "Oh, I could see well enough to see people."

"Did you notice whether she had any bruises on her body?"

DiGiamberardino responded, "No, she had no bruises on her."

As part of the prosecution's and defense's presentations of their conflicting cases, more mind-numbing medical details and theories of Patty's death, the alcohol, the drugs, and the autopsy and toxicology tests that followed had to be presented to the jury. Numerous people that had provided the police with information during their investigation were called to testify at the trial; some had also testified at the preliminary hearing.

There were the doctors who testified in detail at the preliminary hearing and were now put on the stand at the trial, along with additional doctors, for the purpose of offering yet more detailed medical testimony. The prosecution and defense seemed to be trying their cases solely on the minute medical details and theories. People who sat in the witness stand and faced defense attorney Dimitriou were grilled and forced to recollect and repeat facts with no hesitation and certainly no contradiction with what they had previously asserted months or years prior. He rooted out any conflicting testimony and pounced on it with enthusiastic zeal to discredit an adversarial witness.

On February 4, Doctor George H. Kershner, director of emergency medicine at Reading Hospital, was called to the witness stand.

Starting his shift at 8 a.m. on November 27, he received the body of Patricia Gilmore around 9:30 a.m. He immediately examined the body and pronounced her dead. Kershner did not perform any medical assistance because the body was DOA— dead on arrival.

Charles Mackin asked Kershner, "At that time did you state a cause of death?"

Kershner said he did not. When Mackin asked him if he ordered any further testing, he replied, "As I recall, I had a discussion with the coroner at that time, and an autopsy was ordered. I don't recall if I requested it. At this date I don't recall that. But an autopsy was ordered."

Kershner responded to Mackin wanting to know how long the body was in the emergency room. "I can't answer that exactly. The normal procedure would be a half an hour or less. And I don't recall if it was within that time frame of not." The body was then taken to the morgue.

Mackin asked, "While the body was in the emergency room, did you conduct any visual examination?" Kershner said he did, that is routine. Mackin wanted to know what he observed.

Kershner said she was lying on her back with purple discoloration and swelling of the front part of her body when she was brought into the emergency room.

"We rolled her on her side, on either side, just make a visual inspection. And that's when I saw the bloodstains on the panties."

Mackin asked, "Now, did you conduct any further examination based upon what you observed on the panties?"

Kershner answered, "Yes, sir. We lowered the panties. And there were several puncture wounds. I don't recall how many, but there were several puncture wounds on the upper part of the right buttock." Kershner confirmed that the wounds corresponded to the bloodstains on the panties.

Kershner stated that later in the afternoon he went down in the basement to the morgue and attended part of the autopsy, which was already in progress when he got there. Now the body was still lying on its back and the purple discoloration had changed in position, because the body had been lying on its back now for some time. And the purplish discoloration was toward the back of the body now, caused by gravity, and much less in the front, causing the natural skin color to return to the body.

Mackin asked, "And did you notice anything at that point?"

Kershner said, "There was a bruise in the face, a small bruise. And, as I recall, it was, I believe, beneath the right eye."

Kershner said that during the autopsy he observed some blood underneath the scalp, between the scalp and the skull. Kershner said he did not notice any bruises on the face when the body was brought into the emergency room.

Mackin asked, "Based upon your medical knowledge, do you have an explanation for that?"

Kershner explained, "I suspect that the victim died in the prone position, that is face down. And the swelling and discoloration, the purple discoloration, was a result of the position that the body was in for a time. And after the body was on its back for a period of time, several hours, until the autopsy was performed, that discoloration left the front part of the body; and the bruise was a bit more apparent than it was apparent initially."

At this time Judge Schaeffer asked, "Doctor, so I'm clear, when you first saw the body when it was brought into the emergency room, was it lying face up or face down?"

Kershner replied, "Face up when it arrived in the emergency room, Your Honor."

Judge Schaeffer then asked, "So then if the body had been lying face down, would that have been sometime before it was brought into the emergency room?"

Kershner said, "Yes, sir."

Kershner further explained that at the time of death gravity would more or less pull the blood and body fluids toward the more dependent portion of the body. If the body was lying face down, gravity would pull all the blood from the back part of the body down, and conversely when the body would be turned onto its back. The bruises were not noticed when the body was brought into the emergency room because it had been lying in the prone position for such time that the front part of the body had purple discoloration. After the body was placed on its back, as it was in the autopsy room, it took several hours for the blood and fluids to settle to the back of the body, making the bruises visible.

On cross-examination, Dimitriou went over every detail of Doctor Kershner's testimony, questioning the times of events, and especially the position of the body during each phase of it being received by the hospital, and the eventual autopsy.

Dimitriou did ask Kershner who else came to the emergency room when the Muhlenberg Ambulance brought in the body.

Kershner responded, "The ambulance personnel. I believe there was a police officer or detective from the Muhlenberg Police Department, also."

Dimitriou then wanted to know about the conversations he had with the various people in the room. At this time Mackin objected, saying whom Kershner talked to was relevant testimony only if each person was specifically named. Schaeffer sustained Mackin's objection, and asked Kershner whom the conversations were with.

Dimitriou asked, "What was the conversation related to?"

Again Mackin objected. Schaeffer sustained that objection also.

Dimitriou asked, "In any event, Doctor Kershner, you are saying now that you did have a conversation with the police officer in the emergency room?"

"I believe—I recall speaking with him, yes."

Dimitriou then asked, "Do you remember testifying on August the 10th, 1981, that you had no conversations with any police officers?"

Kershner said he didn't recall that. Dimitriou produced the transcript of Kershner's testimony where he said he didn't recall any other conversation between him and another one of the police officers.

Dimitriou asked, "Was there more than one police officer there?"

Kershner replied, "I recall someone showing me a syringe. I thought that was a police officer, and I believe I testified that someone showed me a syringe. At the time—I honestly don't remember with whom I was speaking."

Dimitriou wanted to know if the person Kershner thought was a police officer was in uniform. Kershner said he didn't recall if he was in uniform or not.

Dimitriou asked, "In any event, he showed you a syringe?"

Kershner replied, "Yes, sir."

Kershner confirmed that was the extent of the conversation.

Earlier, ambulance technician Lucille Genslinger had testi-fied that Patty's body was lying face up when she first saw it. Genslinger also said she did not notice any bruises on Patty's face. And Muhlenberg Patrolman Thomas P. Dougherty testi-fied he saw her lying face up when he responded to the scene.

Under direct questioning by Mackin, Doctor John Keith, no longer a pathologist employed by Reading Hospital, ex-plained how his autopsy on Patty Gilmore proceeded on the afternoon of November 27.

Doctor Keith would once again become a pivotal witness, having been questioned extensively at the preliminary hearing. Now his testimony at that hearing would be rehashed and each minute detail examined.

He was employed by the Reading Hospital from May 1973 until the end of June 1984.

Mackin questioned Keith about his duties at the Reading Hospital.

"They were performance of surgical pathology, cytology, and autopsies."

Judge Schaeffer interrupted, "For my benefit, Doctor, what's cytology?"

Keith said, "Cytology is the examination of cellular specimens, principally gynecologic specimens often known as Pap smears."

Mackin asked, "And what else? Autopsies of something else?"

Keith explained, "Autopsies and—not as a function of the pathologist at the Reading Hospital, but independently I would perform on a rotation basis coroner's autopsies."

Mackin continued, "Okay. So let's get back to November 27, 1980. Were you working that day as a pathologist at the Reading Hospital?"

Keith answered, "That was Thanksgiving Day, which was, of course, a holiday at the hospital. And I was on call for whatever autopsies might be requested on that day."

He explained that being on call meant he was not physically in attendance at the hospital, and if there was an autopsy to be performed either at the request of a physician in the hospital or at the request of the coroner, he would be notified and report to the hospital to perform it.

Keith said he was contacted on November 27, and then went to the autopsy room and began an autopsy on Patricia Gilmore sometime that afternoon—it was before 4 p.m.

Mackin asked, "Upon arriving, was there a body there?"

Keith said, "Yes. The body was already in the room where the autopsy was performed."

Mackin asked, "Do you recall how the body was on the autopsy table? Facing up or facing down?"

Keith replied, "Facing up."

Doctor Keith said that prior to beginning the autopsy he did an external examination of the body.

Mackin asked, "Anything observed?"

Keith's response was, "On her face she had an—obvious—"

Now Dimitriou asked Judge Schaeffer to instruct Doctor Keith to simply testify to what he observed without characterizing.

Judge Schaeffer said, "All right. Mr. Dimitriou would like you to leave out the adjectives."

Keith responded, "Fine. Well, fresh is also an adjective, but it's characterization."

Judge Schaeffer replied, "I think you can give that in your opinion. As to what is obvious is more or less up to the individual who may see it. But as a doctor, you certainly say whether it's fresh or not fresh if that relates to your medical experience."

With that said by the judge, Keith replied, "Yes, a fresh, swollen bruising of this region of the face [*indicating*], on the right-hand side right above the zeugmatic arch here, associated with black discoloration of the lower eyelid, known in common parlance as a black eye."

Also, there was a bruise on her nose, a small bruise on her left chin, and one on the top of her left hand. He testified that the bruise on her cheek was caused before death—about four hours before—because it had swollen. Had it been done after she had died, there would not have been swelling, he said.

Keith said he also observed on the right side of her blue panties several reddish, circular stains, suggesting to him they were bloodstains. He said they all measured less than an inch in diameter, and they were grouped fairly close together.

Mackin asked, "Did you, Doctor, then remove the panties from the body?"

He said he did, and explained what he noticed after removing them. "In that same region of the right buttock just beneath where the red staining of the underpants there were four discernible needle marks and a questionable fifth needle mark." Keith confirmed that he found no additional needle marks, and while he was present, photographs were taken of the buttocks area and the needle marks. He said he noticed that the needle marks on the buttock had been directed forward toward the head and were recent because the blood on the surface of the skin was still moist.

While completing the external examination of the body he didn't notice any other needle marks, but did notice a small reddish-colored bruise on the top of the body's left hand.

Before Keith conducted the internal examination of the body, including the body's organs, chest, and abdominal cavity, he testified that he telephoned Gilmore for information as to the circumstances of Patty Gilmore's death, and anything Gilmore could inform him about. Keith said he talked to Gilmore by telephone a few times during the autopsy. When he questioned Gilmore about the bruises, Gilmore said his wife was strongly under the influence of alcohol and had fallen here and there. Keith said Gilmore told him about the evening's activities, especially the drinking, that he went to bed about 1:00 a.m., that Patty came to bed about 2:00 a.m., and how he awoke in the morning and found her lying next to him dead.

Keith said, "The next time I spoke with him would have been after I had examined the internal organs, as well as the scalp, skull, and brain."

Keith said he found no more than an ounce of vomit in

her throat. Keith stressed that choking on the stomach contents could not have caused death.

Mackin asked, "Doctor Keith, do you have an opinion as to whether or not the amount of vomitus that you found in the esophagus of the decedent was of sufficient amount to have caused her death? Do you have such an opinion?"

Keith replied, "Absolutely not." He continued, "Food in the esophagus or vomitus in the esophagus cannot cause or in any way interfere with the vital function of the body. It is in the digestive tract. It cannot in any way interfere with respiration or the function of the body." Responding to Mackin's further inquiry, Keith repeated, "It could absolutely not have caused her death."

Keith continued the autopsy following routine standards and practices such as saving specimens for eventual toxicological examination. Blood and urine samples were saved, along with gastric contents, a portion of the liver and a kidney. He examined the heart and lungs, and the cardiovascular system.

Mackin asked, "And, Doctor Keith, so as far as any of the organs in the body systems that you examined during the course of this autopsy, were any of them, in your opinion, in a condition which would have caused the death of Patricia Gilmore?" Keith replied, "I found no anatomic cause of death."

Next he saw fresh hemorrhages on the front and back of her skull on the undersurface of the scalp while examining her brain. Keith said the amount of blood showed the hemorrhaging occurred before death.

Mackin questioned Keith about the second telephone conversation he had with Gilmore.

Keith responded, "This is a conversation that we've also already discussed. And as I mentioned, I—it would have been after I had examined all of the internal organs, including the head and brain."

Mackin continued, "And what, if anything, did you discuss with Doctor Gilmore during that conversation?"

Keith said, "I mentioned to him that I had found a prominent bruise on the face and possibly two other bruises or two other bruises on the nose, as well as a small bruise on the hand and finally two bruises of the scalp. And I inquired if he had any idea how these might have been incurred."

Mackin asked, "Did he respond?"

Keith said, "He told me that she was strongly under the influence of alcohol and that she was falling here and there."

Mackin asked if Gilmore wanted to talk about the needle marks on the buttocks. Keith said he couldn't remember any specific comments Gilmore made about the needle marks.

To help determine the cause of death Keith sent a blood sample to the hospital's laboratory to establish blood-alcohol content. He sent another blood sample to an outsource laboratory to establish a meperidine level. Samples were also frozen and placed in the hospital morgue's freezer.

The tissue samples that he removed from the buttocks area containing the needle marks, the muscles, the fat, etc., were also frozen and placed in the morgue's freezer. All the blood and tissue samples were put into bags and properly labeled.

Keith said that about a month after he performed the autopsy, he gave the tissue samples to Muhlenberg Police Detective Hadley and Chief Smith.

The defense now began to question star defense expert medical witness Doctor Rudiger Breitenecker, a pathologist on the staff of Baltimore Medical Center in Baltimore, Maryland.

Dimitriou began his questioning by establishing Doctor

Breitenecker's specialty and subspecialties within the specialty of pathology, realizing it all begins with a medical degree.

The doctor testified, "But when you specialize, you take special training in a given field, whatever it may be. And I chose pathology, which is laboratory medicine and examining of bodies and tissues and so forth. And then I became a specialist in that pathology which is anatomic pathology for the tissue part and clinical pathologist for the chemical testing and blood smears, and that sort of thing. Those are two very common subspecialties in pathology.

But then, in addition to that, I subspecialized in forensic medicine and forensic pathology, which is essentially the field of medicine and pathology as applied to the law, to interpret the findings. And, of course, we're concerned with a situation like this today.

Then I also specialized in blood banking as a fourth subspecialty."

Dimitriou asked, "How many pathologists have subspecialties in all four of those subspecialities?"

"Actually this isn't very common. Quite a few pathologists have three subspecialties. But in those four that I'm specialized in, I think I'm the only one east of the Mississippi."

Breitenecker testified that he graduated from the University of Vienna in Austria in 1954. In 1955 he came to America and interned and took a year of surgical training in Michigan. Later he moved to Cleveland, Ohio, and became a board-certified specialist in pathology before joining the teaching staff and fellowship at Duke University.

In 1962 he was appointed assistant medical examiner for the state of Maryland. He became a pathologist and associate directory of laboratories at the Greater Baltimore Medical

Center beginning in 1967. At that time he was also serving as deputy medical examiner for sudden death and criminal death cases such as rape and murder in Baltimore County, Maryland.

Doctor Breitenecker said, "So then in 1975 I was ready to start a rape crisis center of which I'm the director currently and have seen close to a thousand rape cases which I examined and worked on in our rape center which is the center for the county. The reason I bring this up is that part of being a forensic pathologist is to interpret wounds and to look at the body and see what you find and see if the pattern of what you see can be applied to the action at hand. And, of course, with a number of rape victims, you have bruising and so forth to interpret. But this is just sort of to illustrate that I have continued in forensic pathology for the last twenty-five years, let's say."

Doctor Breitenecker's further qualifications include lecturing at Johns Hopkins University, assistant professor of pathology at the University of Maryland, and agent professor of justice administration at the University of Louisville, Kentucky. He published numerous articles, mostly in the field of forensic pathology.

Dimitriou asked, "And have you testified in cases involving trauma, deaths, etc., for the commonwealth? For the prosecution? For the defense?"

Breitenecker responded, "Well, more often for the prosecution. But in recent years also for the defense. I mean, before that as a medical examiner, you just by the nature of the work, you testified for the prosecution. And currently I testify for the prosecution in 99 percent of the rape cases, for instance. But other than that, I testify for whoever needs my interpretation. And if I think there's some merit in the case, I take it, if I see the need for it."

Dimitriou got the doctor to look at a photograph of the

bruise on Patty's left hand. He agreed that it was a mild bruise with a small amount of swelling. When asked if the bruise was inflicted before or after death he responded, "From the picture, impossible to tell. I would say it could be either."

As far as the bruise on the body's forehead, Doctor Breitenecker described it as minute, less than the size of a fingernail. He said it didn't compare to a real bruise, it's more like an accidental bump resulting from a very mild blow.

Dimitriou asked, "Doctor, in all these questions where I'm asking you to repeat an opinion, without me having to repeat it, are these opinions with a reasonable degree of medical certainty?"

The doctor responded, "I wouldn't say them otherwise."

Dimitriou showed Breitenecker another photograph, this time a facial view of the body.

Breitenecker offered his opinion: "This appears to be a left facial view of the deceased. And it shows some brownish and maybe some slight purplish-brownish discoloration on the side of the nose in the linear fashion, possibly with a little scraped part of the linear mark. There is no ruler in the picture. But, I mean, if we picture a nose, I would say—I can't look at my own nose—but I would say half an inch maybe." Breitenecker added that there was no swelling around it.

Dimitriou's next question, "In your opinion, with a reasonable degree of medical certainty, is that bruise premortem or postmortem?" The doctor replied, "I suppose it could be either. However, I favor postmortem because there's no swelling associated with it. It's linear. It doesn't fit anything I can think of that would hit in this area. And so, to me, this is more consistent with a pressure mark that could have happened after death with a nose lying on a slat of some sort."

Dimitriou pointed out that some autopsy tables have slats. "In other words, caused by the—If the autopsy table were a metal table, would that—"

Breitenecker interrupted, "Yeah, that's what I'm talking about. I mean, obviously we know what autopsy tables look like. And some of them have slats. And this could easily be—and somewhere in the protocol it says something about a bent nose. So you can have that. And we already heard time and time again that her face was purple at one time. So some of the purpleness could be just a little left over from that. So I would say in all probability I would rate this as after death. Can't totally exclude the premortem."

Breitenecker reiterated that the mark was consistent with a postmortem injury. Responding to Dimitriou's inquiry, he emphasized that the mark was not caused by a blow to the face by a fist.

"No, it's not consistent with that. Because the other side of the nose, which is in the next picture, shows the symmetrical lesion to this. And you can't hit somebody from both sides into the nose and not bruise it or break the delicate bones of the nose that break like nothing if you hit them and leave a mark like this. So it just does not add up to a blow with the tip totally uninvolved. It makes no sense. You can't hit somebody and cause little scratches and nothing else."

Breitenecker described the mark on the other side of the nose as an even more superficial linear mark, consistent with pressure against it rather than impact. "But again, I am not convinced at all that it is premortem. I think it's postmortem. Because I cannot figure out how it got there without any other damage. But in addition to this, we have a small collection of deep purple blood on the inner third or so of the right lower eyelid. And then below that over the right cheek we have a sutured, meaning sewn-up, incision. And this particular picture doesn't show any discoloration, but I'm told that this was sort of bluish and swollen."

Doctor Breitenecker emphasized that the discoloration in the right eye should not be described as a *black eye*, or *shiner*. Rather this is a collection of blood without swelling on the inner aspect of the eye. Since there isn't any swelling, the marking can also be easily seen in the eyelid which would be totally shrouded by a swollen eye. He stated that there wasn't the slightest suggestion of a swelling around the eye. "You cannot hit somebody in this area with a fist and produce just this one spot. Impossible."

Dimitriou wanted the doctor's opinion as to what he thought caused the markings on the eye.

"We've seen it time and time again. The cause is that from the swollen area of the cheek while the body was lying down, it trickled and showed up in that area. You see that all the time."

Breitenecker testified that the absence of any swelling in the eyelid made him conclude that the markings were definitely postmortem, postmortem drainage after death and no particular reaction to it.

Dimitriou asked if the facial bruise on the cheek could have been caused by stumbling up the steps.

Breitenecker responded, "Up the steps; down the steps. I mean, anything. When you hit your cheek, you get a bruise if you hit it hard enough. In this case it wasn't hard because it didn't break the skin at all. But bump it, I mean, a bump of some significance to cause a few blood vessels to rupture and, therefore, the swelling to develop. But it didn't break the skin. It didn't leave any marks on the skin. If you say up the steps, which is a possibility because—were the steps carpeted?"

Dimitriou said they were.

"Then well, I think that would make sense. Because I would assume that the impact had to be something cushioned, reasonably soft. Because if you hit the edge of a wooden board or something, you leave a mark in the skin as a rule. So I think this is something hard but that is cushioned. And steps are entirely within the range of that, the edge of a carpeted step.

Dimitriou asked the doctor if he concluded that the cause of Patty Gilmore's death was a combination of Demerol and alcohol.

Breitenecker answered, "It most likely was the cause of death."

Dimitriou asked, "Now can you exclude aspirated vomitus as a cause of death where the pathologist has found a small amount of vomitus in the trachea, in the larynx, and in the bronchi? Can you exclude aspirated vomitus as a cause of death?"

Breitenecker responded, "I can't exclude it, but I would like to see more vomitus in the trachea and bronchi. But we all have seen cases where people, for instance, drown and have no water in their lungs and get a few drops into the voice box, the larynx. And they have a spasm, and they suffocate. So that some people that—well, in this case you have the Demerol and the alcohol already depressing the respiration to begin with, depressing the gag reflex, for instance. And you get wine and stomach acid up and even a small amount that hits the larynx could cause a spasm. So that a small amount could possibly, you know, contribute to aspiration. But this is hard to prove. It's certainly possible. But with the Demerol and the alcohol, I wouldn't look for anything in addition. But if you ask me can I exclude aspiration, no, I can't."

Dimitriou pressed on about the fact that a small amount of vomitus was found in the trachea, the larynx, and the bronchi, and when that is added to the 0.24 blood alcohol plus the level of Demerol found in the blood, can aspirated vomitus be ruled out as a cause of death? Doctor Breitenecker said he couldn't totally exclude it as a reason, but he didn't know if it was necessary to have three causes of death.

The doctor commented, "Well, you know, you have Demerol; you have alcohol. Together we definitely accept this as reasonable cause of death. And I don't know if one has to say well in addition to that now, we need sort of the straw that breaks the camel's back. And that's the aspiration. I cannot say that didn't happen, because we know it was there. But with or without the aspiration, I think she might have died. The aspiration certainly is a possibility of the mechanism of death, also." At this point Breitenecker testified that he thought Patty Gilmore died because of the combination of alcohol and Demerol.

Dimitriou now turned his attention to the syringe and the injections that were placed in Patty's right buttock area.

He asked Breitenecker if he agreed with previous testimony given by Doctor Mihalakis stating that one of the reasons why she could not have self-injected with a syringe with a 0.24 blood alcohol is because the tracks were cephalic and that the natural motion would be in a downward motion.

Dimitriou asked, "In your opinion, would self-injection—would the cephalad trajectory be more compatible with self-injection than not?"

Breitenecker explained, "Yes it would. Because no doctor or nurse ever shoots a needle upwards. I mean it's just not done. I mean you hit it straight on. It never goes up. I mean, I've never, ever seen it. And I've given hundreds of injections and watched a lot. I mean, it's just not done. To shove it up is when you have the syringe between your thumb and third finger and push the plunger up. And it's in a logical direction, assuming that you do it yourself."

Dimitriou pointed out that the needle marks were grouped in two and three, suggesting that it hurts to put an injection in the same area. But Breitenecker said that somebody with an alcohol reading of 0.24 has no pain and wouldn't be concerned at all with pain from a needle.

Dimitriou set his sights on asking a key defense question. He wanted to know whether other sites would be more suitable for self-injection, such as the thighs. "In any event, Doctor, you agree that it could be on the thighs or it could be anyplace; but you can't exclude self-injection?"

Breitenecker quickly responded, "Definitely not. It's not the usual location though."

Dimitriou asked the doctor if he agreed that meperidine and alcohol are additives, and enhance a person's chance of stumbling and falling when these drugs were in the system. He also wanted to know about the effects if Lomotil was also in the person's system.

Breitenecker said, "Well, that just adds to it. Lomotil and meperidine or Demerol are known to be—in some of the textbooks they call them almost a dangerous combination because one sort of enhances the other. And you may get unsuspected effects from it."

Judge Schaeffer wanted to know if the Lomotil had been in the body at a therapeutic level only, would it still have a dangerous additive effect? Breitenecker stated that he thought it would.

Next Dimitriou tackled the question of the bruises on the body.

"Now, Doctor, Mr. Mihalakis has testified that singly all these marks or bruises that have been testified to could be caused by various number of ways. However, in his opinion, they were not caused by stumbling or falling or any other way if they were premortem, if we accept his premise that they were premortem. Because they were collective.

"Do you have an opinion to his—when he says that these are collective and for that reason they could not be blows—I mean they could be blows rather than some other cause which they could be singly?"

Breitenecker reiterated his previous testimony about the various marks on the body. Then he said, "As a matter of fact, I didn't mention that. But if I may, Demerol overdose can give you seizures. This is a very well recognized complication of a Demerol overdose, that you start seizing. And if she was in bed and she banged it against the headboard, —I don't know what the bed looks like—"

Breitenecker said that he disagreed with Doctor Mihalakis, he did not consider the marks as being collective. In other words, he believed the marks were made over a period of time as opposed to resulting from injuries incurred at the same time, perhaps inflicted during an altercation.

During cross-examination, Mackin came out swinging.

"Now doctor, you do have an opinion, do you not, to a reasonable degree of certainty, as to cause of death in this case?"

Breitenecker answered, "As we've said about ten times before, it's the combination of Demerol and alcohol which we have put in the forefront."

Mackin came back, "But it's not aspiration of vomitus, in your opinion?"

Breitenecker said, "I consider this a less well documented possibility. But I can't exclude it, as I said."

Mackin asked, "Well, is it your opinion that she died from a combination of meperidine and alcohol or is it your opinion that she died from a combination of meperidine, alcohol, and aspirated vomitus?"

Breitenecker answered, "Either way you want it, it would be acceptable. Absolutely."

So Mackin pointed out that evidently Breitenecker had two opinions of how Patty Gilmore died. Breitenecker said that his two opinions were identical except one is a little expanded over the other. He did not feel the two opinions contradicted at all.

Mackin got Doctor Breitenecker to conclude that, based on the toxicology report being accurate, Patty Gilmore had a Demerol overdose. However Breitenecker still maintained that the bruising on the body occurred postmortem, after death.

Mackin asked, "Now Doctor, you testified earlier that at 0.24 she was a stumbling drunk?"

Breitenecker reacted, "She could have been, yes, depending on how used she was to alcohol. I mean, there are some people that don't stumble." He said that with a 0.24 reading and Demerol in her bloodstream, she would be stumbling in all probability.

Mackin asked, "How long does it take Demerol to get into the—let's assume an inter-muscular injection, how long does it take Demerol to get into the blood?"

Breitenecker replied, "Less than a half hour, maybe fifteen minutes. I mean it gets in the blood right away." He said that's when it would start mixing with the alcohol when it's all circulating throughout the whole body.

The doctor said he had prepared to testify by reviewing pertinent medical information. He stated he reviewed the autopsy report, the laboratory findings, preliminary hearing transcripts of testimony by doctors Keith, Mihalakis, Kershner, and Rieders, plus a 1980 taped transcript of Doctor Keith, transcripts of the trial currently taking place, and the photographs that had been presented as evidence to the court. He said that with a reasonable degree of medical certainty, Patty Gilmore had overdosed on Demerol.

Breitenecker repeated, "If the toxicology report is correct, then it would be an overdose."

The cross-examination continued, rehashing the discoloration of the body that occurred during the autopsy, and the bruises that were either caused premortem or postmortem.

Mackin now asked, "Doctor Breitenecker, have you many autopsies in which the cause of death was an overdose of meperidine and alcohol?"

Breitenecker responded, "I don't remember doing any."

Mackin said, "You don't remember doing any?"

"No, I looked through the records. Our office in Baltimore, the medical examiner, is where I work."

Mackin asked, "But you, yourself, Doctor, meperidine, Demerol, alcohol. Then the cause of death in a person like Patricia Gilmore would affect the respiratory system of the central nervous system and then her breathing would be more shallow, more shallow, and then pass away?"

Breitenecker responded, "Essentially. Sometimes with seizures."

Judge Schaeffer wanted to know what he meant by "sometimes."

Breitenecker said, "Seizures. And that's logical again. Because you breathe slower and shallow. The brain doesn't get oxygen, and this is one way of getting seizures that the brain is deprived of enough oxygen. And that's very common."

Mackin inquired about congestion that is common in drug-related deaths.

Breitenecker explained, "Congestion means that blood pools in blood vessels and they become dilated and even gorged with blood. Congestion may also lead to leakage of fluid, and that leads to fluid or water in the lungs. And then it's congestion of the lung with pulmonary edema. Since you said you want to talk about it sooner or later, I'm just throwing that out as a starting point. So that congestion fills the blood vessels, makes it difficult to breathe because the vessels are sort of sluggish and congested, full of blood, and then they leak and fluid gets into the lung which is a mechanism of death in drug overdoses particularly. Well, you said that yourself. But this is par for the course. I mean, this is very common."

Mackin asked, "So congestion is very common in drug-related deaths?"

Breitenecker replied, "Yes, and also in aspiration of vomitus."

Mackin asked, "And we do have congestion—you've read the autopsy protocol, correct?"

Breitenecker confirmed, "Congestion did exist in the liver and the lungs."

More testimony was given on bruising, particularly the fact that Patty Gilmore's nose was bent, allegedly from being turned over on the autopsy table.

Mackin asked, "Doctor, postmortem injuries, that's what I'd like to talk about right now. In your opinion, are bruises to the nose, to the eye, or purple discoloration, the one on the nasal aspect of the eye, are such markings rare?"

Breitenecker's reply: "Yes."

Mackin asked, "Okay. As a matter of fact, Doctor, would this be a fair statement, that the textbooks say that bruising does not occur postmortem?"

Breitenecker answered, "The less voluminous textbooks would certainly say that, who concentrate on the great majority of cases and don't necessarily elucidate also-occurring rare ones."

Judge Schaeffer asked, "Okay, Doctor, whether they occur in these rare ones, if you know this, is there a particular cause for that, like a disease a person might have been suffering from?"

Breitenecker said, "No. No. A cause where we see rarely but not more often? Well, I don't think there's a particular cause unless you want to say cause is the disruption of a blood vessel after death with depending blood oozing into it."

Schaeffer asked, "Well, my question was, in these rare cases that the deceased had been, for instance, a hemophiliac, would that make it more likely that there would be postmortem bruising?"

Breitenecker said, "I don't know. I don't think so. I don't know."

Schaeffer asked, "And what about somebody suffering from leukemia, would there be more likely to be postmortem bruising?"

Breitenecker responded, "They bruise antemortem very easily. But postmortem—I think gravity is the same for everybody as long as there's blood to settle, you know."

Breitenecker explained, after Schaeffer asked him if he knew, that he saw no way how a disease could really make such a difference.

Mackin asked, "So less voluminous textbooks teach that?"

Breitenecker responded, "Yes."

Mackin, wanting to get a precise response, asked, "Bruising does not occur postmortem?"

Breitenecker replied, "Yes."

Mackin asked, "Let me just ask you. Do you recall having a conversation on February 3, 1987, with—that was last week, nine days ago—"

Breitenecker answered, "Yes."

Mackin continued, "—by telephone with a person from my office named Marsha Mills from the Office of Attorney General, Commonwealth of Pennsylvania? I introduced Miss Mills to you."

Breitenecker replied, "Very nice voice."

Mackin went on, "And at that time, Doctor, didn't you tell her that doctors are trained that bruising does not occur postmortem?"

Breitenecker said, "Well, trained or taught. I mean, you know, if you teach medical students who become doctors and so forth, I mean, you don't always use the exception to the rule. And I could mention many different things and that—"

Judge Schaeffer interjected, "The answer is yes or no. Did you tell this young lady? Yes or no."

Breitenecker responded, "I don't know the exact words. But certainly I would agree that I may have said something to the effect that the general teaching is that bruising doesn't occur before—I mean, after death. I mean, this is sort of a standard baseline of forensic pathology. But we always have the exceptions to the rule; and they are not always taught, the fine print, so to say."

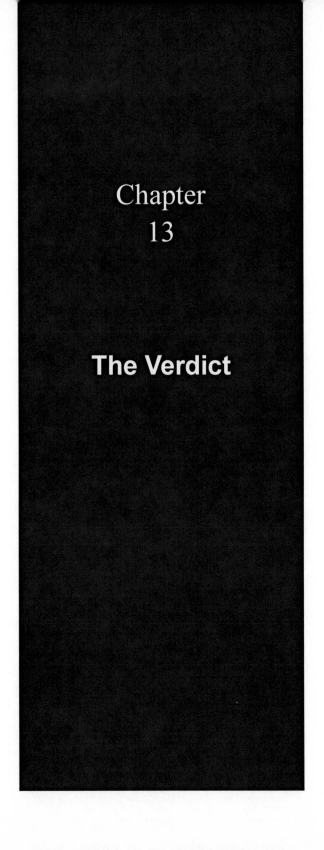

Chapter 13

The Verdict

The prosecution and the Muhlenberg Police believed they had a strong case to convict Doctor Irvin Gilmore of criminal homicide. The doctor had been charged with criminal homicide, aggravated assault, and recklessly endangering another person, and was facing as much as five years in prison. However, most prosecutors and police also believe that no matter how strong the case, you never know what will happen when the fate of a defendant is put in the hands of a jury.

The verdict came in on Friday, February 20, 1987. The jury of his peers decided that the doctor was guilty only of recklessly endangering another person. No conviction of criminal homicide. No conviction of aggravated assault.

And certainly not the sure conviction had the doctor's guilty plea to involuntary manslaughter been accepted by Judge Schaeffer four years earlier.

Guilty of reckless endangerment wasn't the verdict the prosecution had hoped for, but it was a conviction nevertheless.

When court was adjourned members of the jury kissed and hugged Gilmore, even though they had just convicted him of a serious crime. Later Gilmore said he would appeal the decision, but Dimitriou was not overly concerned about the verdict.

When asked after the trial to comment, Dimitriou repeated his contention that he had made in court that the doctor, because he still made house calls, would frequently leave his medical bag in the back seat of his car, and that Patty Gilmore could have taken the bag out of the car while her husband slept, and injected herself in the buttocks.

A person commits the crime of reckless endangerment if the accused recklessly engages in conduct which creates a substantial risk of serious physical injury to another person. "Reckless" conduct is conduct that exhibits a culpable disregard of foreseeable consequences to others from the act or omission involved. The accused need not intentionally cause resulting harm. To get a conviction the court must believe that the accused's conduct put another person in imminent danger. The ultimate question is whether the accused's conduct made it actually or imminently dangerous to the rights or safety of others.

A year later, in February 1988, Judge Schaeffer sentenced Gilmore to two years of probation, 200 hours of community service, and a $3,000 fine.

Did Doctor Gilmore inject his wife with Demerol? He admitted he had. Did he inject her with an *accidental* overdose? Was there any available evidence to prove he killed her intentionally? Muhlenberg Police Chief Harley Smith was convinced he deliberately killed her, but his small police force didn't have the resources to effectively investigate and attempt to prove their case.

Plenty of questions will always remain unanswered. Gilmore claimed he didn't remember anything that happened when Patty came to bed because he was overcome with fatigue and alcohol.

Perhaps he became suspicious and suddenly jealous as a result of Patty staying out until 3 a.m. early Wednesday after teaching a CPR class. She told him she had car trouble. Gilmore stated when interviewed that he waited up all night for her to get home, and didn't sleep the rest of that early Wednesday morning after she finally did arrive home. A confrontation and altercation could have occurred at that time that resulted in bruises on her body—the bruises that appeared during the pre-autopsy examination. Could they have hidden the quarreling and bruises from his visiting son and daughter-in-law?

Could he have suddenly had an emotional breakdown as a result of this sudden jealousy after he retired alone to his bedroom Thanksgiving eve? When Patty finally came to bed and passed out or fell asleep, he wouldn't have been able to give her a clean injection if he was weeping and his arm shaking from grief. The result could have been an increased risk of overdose and the multiple needle marks that turned up during the autopsy.

Multiple needle marks would have also resulted if Gilmore killed Patty while he was drunk, again not realizing how many times and how much of what drug he was injecting into her with an unsteady hand.

If Gilmore intentionally injected Patty with an overdose of Demerol, he was certainly smart enough to realize that injecting her multiple times would depict self-injection and certainly not injections he, an experienced medical doctor, would give her.

Of course, it is possible that Patty Gilmore did in fact inject herself with Demerol while drunk; not realizing it was the drug she feared. However, the cephalad trajectory and the number of needle marks that would point to self-injection remain open to debate.

There is absolutely no indication or suspicion that Patty's death was a suicide.

In the fall of 1988 a hearing examiner ruled that Gilmore did not have to surrender his medical license, but should be reprimanded. The Pennsylvania Department of State appealed that decision, resulting in the Pennsylvania State Board of Medicine suspending his license for two years. Gilmore agreed to surrender his license at that time. The board had waited until the criminal case was complete before taking action.

Gilmore reached a settlement in September 1991 with the board of medicine to permanently revoke his medical license as of December 10, 1991. He then changed his mind and appealed to Commonwealth Court and the board to reinstate his license.

In a legal notice published in the *Reading Eagle* on October 10, 1991, the board notified any interested parties of its order revoking the license to practice medicine of Doctor Irvin Gilmore. It went on to say the revocation was based upon his misdemeanor conviction of recklessly endangering the life of another person and his *improper administration* to his wife Patricia on November 27, 1980, an unknown life-threatening amount of the drug Demerol, which resulted in her death.

In January 1992 Gilmore retired from practicing medicine and gave up the fight to prevent his license from being permanently revoked. He claimed he was withdrawing his appeal because he didn't want to relive his wife's death and he believed the strain of the litigation necessary to carry on the fight would be too much for him to handle. By that time he had remarried and had turned his medical practice over to another physician.

Gilmore died in Berks County, Pennsylvania, on September 2, 2002, at age 80. According to his obituary published in the *Reading Eagle* on September 3, 2002, he was survived by his son Barry. Other survivors included a sister.

He was entombed next to Patty in the Laureldale Cemetery Mausoleum, Tuckerton, Pennsylvania, just a couple of miles from the house they shared on Kutztown Road in Temple, Pennsylvania.

CPSIA information can be obtained at www.ICGtesting.com
Printed in the USA
BVOW010334051212

307354BV00001B/4/P